ACOUSTIC GUITAR MAGAZINE'S

private lessons

FINGERSTYLE GUITAR ESSENTIALS

STRING LETTER PUBLISHING

Publisher: David A. Lusterman

Editor: Jeffrey Pepper Rodgers

Managing Editor, Special Products: David Johnson

Music Editor: Dylan Schorer

Designer: Elena Tapiero Brown

Desktop Publishing Technician: Lisa Brazieal

Production Coordinator: Christi Payne

Music Engraving: Dylan Schorer

Cover Photo: Peter Figen

Photographs: Rob Thomas (Dix Bruce), Ben Ailes (Dale Miller), Willie Floyd (Dylan Schorer)

Library of Congress Cataloging-in-Publication Data

Fingerstyle guitar essentials.
        p.   cm. — (Acoustic guitar magazine's private lessons)
    Includes music.
    ISBN 1-890490-06-7 (alk. paper)
    1. Guitar—Instruction and study.   I. Series.
MT580.F42   1998
787.87' 19368—dc21   98-37042
                          CIP
                         MN

STRING LETTER PUBLISHING

contents

CD track list

introduction

Playing fingerstyle is one of the most beautiful ways to coax music out of an acoustic guitar. A rolling fingerpicking pattern behind a singer is one of the most appealing accompaniments around. Fingerpicking is one of the most effective ways to create a solo guitar style; you can break away from single line runs or chord strumming and create music with independent bass lines, melodies, and chords. There's also something about the tactile satisfaction earned by plucking the strings with your fingers.

In this book, we present 12 in-depth lessons from the master teachers at *Acoustic Guitar* magazine on all aspects of fingerstyle guitar playing, from basic techniques to arranging to using alternate tunings. And all of the techniques discussed are backed up with "real-world" musical examples showing how you can apply these ideas to your playing right away. Each section of the book progresses from introductory material to lessons that require some technical skill and knowledge. If you're unfamiliar with any terms or techniques used, check the music notation key. Whether you've only been playing guitar a short time, or you're an old pro looking for some new tricks, you're sure to find many ways to improve your playing and musicality in these pages.

Dylan Schorer
Music Editor, *Acoustic Guitar*

music notation key

The music in this book is written in standard notation and tablature. Here's how to read it.

STANDARD NOTATION

Standard notation is written on a five-line staff. Notes are written in alphabetical order from A to G.

The duration of a note is determined by three things: the note head, stem, and flag. In 4/4 time whole note (○) equals four beats. A half note (♩) is half of that: two beats. A quarter note (♩) equals one beat, an eighth note (♪) equals half of one beat, and a 16th note (♫) is a quarter beat (there are four 16th notes per beat).

The fraction (4/4, 3/4, 6/8, etc.) or ¢ character shown at the beginning of a piece of music denotes the time signature. The top number tells you how many beats are in each measure, and the bottom number indicates the rhythmic value of each beat (4 equals a quarter note, 8 equals an eighth note, 16 equals a 16th note, and 2 equals a half note). The most common time signature is 4/4, which signifies four quarter notes per measure and is sometimes designated with the symbol ¢ (for common time). The symbol ¢ stands for cut time (2/2). Most songs are either in 4/4 or 3/4.

TABLATURE

In tablature, the six horizontal lines represent the six strings of the guitar, with the first string on the top and sixth on the bottom. The numbers refer to fret numbers on a given string. The notation and tablature in this book are designed to be used in tandem—refer to the notation to get the rhythmic information and note durations, and refer to the tablature to get the exact locations of the notes on the guitar fingerboard.

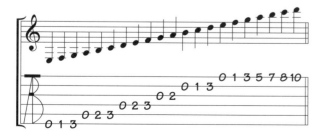

FINGERINGS

Fingerings are indicated with small numbers and letters in the notation. Fretting-hand fingering is indicated with 1 for the index finger, 2 the middle, 3 the ring, 4 the pinky, and *T* the thumb. Picking-hand fingering is indicated by *i* for the index finger, *m* the middle, *a* the ring, *c* the pinky, and *p* the thumb. Remember that the fingerings indicated are only suggestions; if you find a different way that works better for you, use it.

CHORD DIAGRAMS

Chord diagrams show where the fingers go on the fingerboard. Frets are shown horizontally. The thick top line represents the nut. A Roman numeral to the right of a diagram indicates a chord played higher up the neck (in this case the top horizontal line is thin). Strings are shown as vertical lines. The line on the far left represents the sixth (lowest) string, and the line on the far right represents the first (highest) string. Dots show where the fingers go, and thick horizontal lines indicate barres. Numbers above the diagram are left-hand finger numbers, as used in standard notation. Again, the fingerings are only suggestions. An *X* indicates a string that should be muted or not played; 0 indicates an open string.

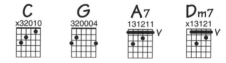

CAPOS

If a capo is used, a Roman numeral indicates the fret where the capo should be placed. The standard notation and tablature is written as if the capo were the nut of the guitar. For instance, a tune capoed anywhere up the neck and played using key-of-G chord shapes and fingerings will be written in the key of G. Likewise, open strings held down by the capo are written as open strings.

TUNINGS

Alternate guitar tunings are given from the lowest (sixth) string to the highest (first) string. For instance, D A D G B E indicates standard tuning with the bottom string dropped to D. Standard notation for songs in alternate tunings always reflects the actual pitches of the notes.

VOCAL TUNES

Vocal tunes are sometimes written with a fully tabbed-out introduction and a vocal melody with chord diagrams for the rest of the piece. The tab intro is usually your indication of which strum or fingerpicking pattern to use in the rest of the piece. The melody with lyrics underneath is the melody sung by the vocalist. Occasionally smaller notes are written with the melody to indicate the harmony part sung by another vocalist. These are not to be confused with cue notes, which are small notes that indicate melodies that vary when a section is repeated. Listen to a recording of the piece to get a feel for the guitar accompaniment and to hear the singing if you aren't skilled at reading vocal melodies.

ARTICULATIONS

There are a number of ways you can articulate a note on the guitar. Notes connected with slurs (not to be confused with ties) in the tablature or standard notation are articulated with either a hammer-on, pull-off, or slide. Lower notes slurred to higher notes are played as hammer-ons; higher notes slurred to lower notes are played as pull-offs. While it's usually obvious that slurred notes are played as hammer-ons or pull-offs, an *H* or *P* is included above the tablature as an extra reminder.

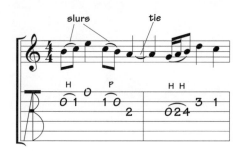

Slides are represented with a dash, and an *S* is included above the tab. A dash preceding a note represents a slide into the note from an indefinite point in the direction of the slide; a dash following a note indicates a slide off of the note to an indefinite point in the direction of the slide. For two slurred notes connected with a slide, you should pick the first note and then slide into the second.

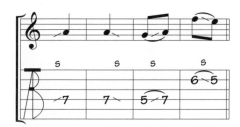

Bends are represented with upward curves, as shown in the next example. Most bends have a specific destination pitch—

the number above the bend symbol shows how much the bend raises the string's pitch: ¼ for a slight bend, ½ for a half step, 1 for a whole step.

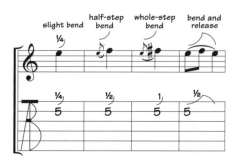

HARMONICS

Harmonics are represented by diamond-shaped notes in the standard notation and a small dot next to the tablature numbers. Natural harmonics are indicated with the text "Harmonics" or "Harm." above the tablature. Harmonics articulated with the right hand (often called artificial harmonics) include the text "R.H. Harmonics" or "R.H. Harm." above the tab. Right-hand harmonics are executed by lightly touching the harmonic node (usually 12 frets above the open string or fretted note) with the right-hand index finger and plucking the string with the thumb or ring finger or pick. For extended phrases played with right-hand harmonics, the fretted notes are shown in the tab along with instructions to touch the harmonics 12 frets above the notes.

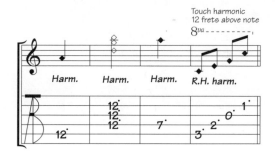

REPEATS

One of the most confusing parts of a musical score can be the navigation symbols, such as repeats, *D.S. al Coda*, *D.C. al Fine*, *To Coda*, etc.

Repeat symbols are placed at the beginning and end of the passage to be repeated.

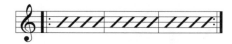

You should ignore repeat symbols with the dots on the right side the first time you encounter them; when you come to a repeat symbol with dots on the left side, jump back to the previous repeat symbol facing the opposite direction (if there is no previous symbol, go to the beginning of the piece). The next time you come to the repeat symbol, ignore it and keep going unless it includes instructions such as "Repeat three times."

A section will often have a different ending after each repeat. The example below includes a first and a second ending. Play until you hit the repeat symbol, jump back to the previous repeat symbol and play until you reach the bracketed first ending, skip the measures under the bracket and jump immediately to the second ending, and then continue.

of the piece when you encounter this indication. Both *D.C.* and *D.S.* are usually accompanied by *al Fine* or *al Coda*. *Fine* indicates the end of a piece. A coda is a final passage near the end of a piece and is indicated with ⊕. *D.S. al Coda* simply tells you to jump back to the sign and continue on until you are instructed to jump to the coda, indicated with *To Coda* ⊕.

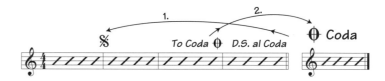

D.S. stands for *dal segno* or "from the sign." When you encounter this indication, jump immediately to the sign (𝄋). *D.C.* stands for *da capo* or "from the beginning." Jump to the top

D.C. al Fine tells you to jump to the beginning of a tune and continue until you encounter the *Fine* indicating the end of the piece (ignore the *Fine* the first time through).

about the teachers

DAVID HAMBURGER

David Hamburger is a guitarist, teacher, and writer who lives in Brooklyn, New York. He plays guitar, Dobro, and pedal steel on his 1994 debut recording, *King of the Brooklyn Delta* (Chester Records, PO Box 170504, Brooklyn, NY 11217) and on many other artists' recordings, including Chuck Brodsky's *Letters in the Dirt* (Red House, 1996). He's a regular teacher at the National Guitar Summer Workshop and the author of several instruction books.

MARK HANSON

Guitarist, publisher, and educator Mark Hanson founded the music publishing company Accent on Music (19363 Willamette Dr. #252, West Linn, OR 97068; [800] 313-4406; [503] 699-1814; www.accentonmusic.com). He is the author of over 20 guitar instruction manuals, arrangement folios, and instructional videos, including the best-selling *Complete Book of Alternate Tunings* (Accent on Music) and *Fingerstyle Wizard* (Warner Bros.), a book and CD of his arrangements of the songs from *The Wizard of Oz*. Hanson has been giving acoustic guitar instructions to classes and seminars nationwide since 1972 and performs with the Acoustic Guitar Summit quartet.

JOHN KNOWLES

In 1996, Chet Atkins awarded John Knowles an honorary CGP degree (Certified Guitar Player) for his work as a guitarist and educator. Knowles has recorded as a soloist and with others including Atkins, Floyd Cramer, and James Galway. He is the author of numerous music books including *Chet Atkins: Note-for-Note, Jerry Reed: Heavy Neckin',* and *Lenny Breau: Fingerstyle Jazz* (Mel Bay). Knowles and Atkins wrote and produced the acclaimed instructional video *Chet Atkins: Get Started on Guitar.* Knowles also writes and publishes *John Knowles' FingerStyle Quarterly* (PO Box 120355, Nashville, TN 37212; [800] 662-0577; johnknowle@aol.com). Each summer, he teaches at several workshops around the country including the Puget Sound Guitar Workshop, the National Guitar Summer Workshop, and the California Coast Music Camp. He is also deputy director of education and research at the Country Music Hall of Fame and Museum in Nashville.

DALE MILLER

Dale Miller is a fingerstyle guitarist, guitar teacher, music store owner, freelance writer, and computer consultant living in Berkeley, California. His earliest guitar idol was John Fahey, and his first solo recording was *Fingerpicking Rags and Other Delights* (re-released by Fantasy Records in 1995). His most recent album, *Both of Me* (Dale Miller Productions), features duets of jazz standards and leads with a National steel guitar. Miller is the author of the book/CD combo *Country Blues and Ragtime Guitar Styles* (Mel Bay Publications).

CHRIS PROCTOR

Chris Proctor is a nationally renowned performer and composer for the steel-string guitar. A former U.S. National Fingerstyle Guitar Champion, he has toured internationally and released five recordings of his original compositions and arrangements and three books of his transcriptions. His most recent album is *Only Now* (Flying Fish). Proctor teaches his techniques through hundreds of guitar workshops.

DYLAN SCHORER

Guitarist Dylan Schorer, *Acoustic Guitar*'s music editor, was the 1993 winner of the fingerpicking contest at the Telluride Bluegrass Festival. He performs throughout the San Francisco Bay Area, accompanying various songwriters and playing solo. He currently plays and records in the Celtic ensemble Logan's Well with guitarist Steve Baughman and vocalist Carleen Duncan.

DICK WEISSMAN

Artist, record producer, songwriter, and author Dick Weissman started playing guitar while a student at Goddard College in Vermont. He studied folk guitar in New York with Jerry Silverman and jazz guitar with Dan Fox and Barry Galbraith. In the 1960s he was a member of the pop-folk group the Journeymen, with John Phillips and Scott McKenzie. They toured North America and recorded three albums for Capitol. Weissman has lived in Colorado since 1973, where he writes instrumental music and teaches classes on the music business and the cultural study of music at the University of Colorado at Denver. He has written six books about music and the music business and has recorded and produced three albums of instrumental music on the Folk Era label, including his new album, *Reflections*. He has also composed two feature film scores.

JIM WOOD

Multi-instrumentalist Jim Wood lives in Fairview, Tennessee, and works as a performer, studio musician, and instructor in Nashville. A fiddler since the age of ten, he has won more than 120 fiddle contests and has recorded with such artists as Ray Price, Emmylou Harris, Mike Snider, John McEuen, Greg Brown, Amy Grant, and many others. Wood also owns and operates his own recording studio. His other musical skills include playing the bouzouki, mandolin, viola, bass, banjo, and bodhran. Wood also has credits for radio and television soundtracks and arrangements with TNN, ESPN, and the Discovery Channel.

Fingerstyle Basics

Chris Proctor

When guitarists are introduced to playing fingerstyle, a certain bewilderment can set in. "You mean I have to sing, change chords, move my thumb back and forth in rhythmically appropriate ways on the bottom three strings of the guitar, and move two or three fingers on the upper strings in a melodically pleasing manner? How am I supposed to learn and coordinate all of these activities? That's at least four different things to think about, right?"

Put aside the confusion that is always rampant when learning a new skill and imagine yourself watching a skillful motorist driving a car with a standard transmission. You're 14 years old, and nothing ever seemed cooler or more unlikely than learning how to drive a standard—your left foot in charge of the clutch but coordinated with your right foot, which has to figure out when to go from gas to brake at the correct time for your right hand, which has to navigate that intricate little diagram on top of the gearshift knob, while your left hand steers the car and your head and eyes make decisions about how fast, what lane, what direction, and so on. Broken down in that manner, driving sounds like a hopelessly complex skill, and it probably seemed so when you were 14.

But what happened? You practiced. You stalled the car a couple of times, but within six months you were not only performing all of the skills flawlessly, but you were balancing a drink in your lap and messing with the cassette player or hunting for acoustic music somewhere in FM land. Best of all, and most significantly for you budding fingerstylists, you actually became a much better driver once you got skillful enough that you no longer needed to think about what you were doing. When you ceased to be preoccupied with learning these new functions assigned to various body parts and they became motor skills, you were free to think about other routes to your destination, traffic, your speed, and possible dangers to your vehicle, and when you did so, your driving improved markedly.

So it is with your hands and fingers in fingerstyle guitar playing. First you will need to put some intensive time into teaching your right hand the different functions required of it, so that you can later rely on it to take care of itself while you focus your attention elsewhere—on your singing, on intricate left-hand fingering, or on the feeling you wish to communicate with your music.

Your right-hand thumb is in charge of keeping the beat, and it must not falter.

Introduction TRACK 2

THE RULE OF THUMB

Your right-hand thumb is king of the hill, in charge of keeping the beat, letting everyone know what chord you're playing by playing tonic notes on strong beats of the measure, and generally being the foundation of the sound. It must not falter. Accordingly, we start by playing with the right thumb alone in an alternating-bass style (see Example 1).

Your right thumb has to know only two things: where the root, or tonic, of the chord is and where the fourth string is. It should alternate between those two strings, with one note on every quarter-note beat. With the exception of the D chord (in which the best option is to play the F♯ note on the bottom E string), all first-position chords will give you a low root on the fifth or sixth string. While all of the exercises for this lesson are written in the key of C, you must be able to play them in every first-position chord and chord progression that you know, so you are sure that your thumb is automatic. Remember, we'll soon be using fingers as well, and changing chords and singing, so the thumb's role has to become second nature.

Example 2 begins the process of adding melody. I generally assign one finger to each string—the index finger to the G string, the middle finger to the B string, and the ring finger to the E string. This particular example uses all three fingers playing whole notes in the beginning of each bar, while the bass continues to do its alternating job. Once again, if you can do this in C, try using a different chord. Make sure that the thumb doesn't waver.

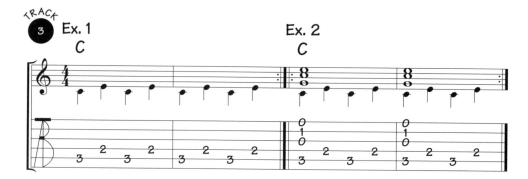

Example 3 gives you two melody notes per measure, while Example 4 provides four such notes, with the bass marching boldly forward as before. These are relatively simple exercises, because your right-hand fingers are not yet being asked to play any notes at different times than your right thumb.

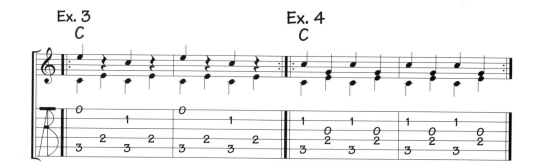

RHYTHMIC INDEPENDENCE

Examples 5 and 6 take that next step. If this is new to you, expect to take some time and care to lock these new skills into place. These are the first exercises that require your thumb and fingers to act with rhythmic independence, and I guarantee that your thumb will behave undependably as you concentrate on these new, more difficult finger motions. Think of these patterns as being composed of two parts, melody and bass, and try them separately before putting the two together. First play just the melody until you can hear it in your head, then try just the bass with your thumb, and finally try them both together.

PLAYING REAL MUSIC

As a reward for your labors, it's time for real music. I have always liked the pretty melody and unusual chord changes (for a traditional folk song) in "Aura Lee," and the song requires only a simple fingerstyle technique based almost entirely upon the preceding exercises. The bass alternates as I have described, and the melody is not fast or tricky. I have kept your inner fingers busy playing extra notes in some places, and if you wish to simplify the song, just play the uppermost melody notes and ignore those below it. Try to learn the tune well enough to play it in the slow, pretty style that it deserves.

Good luck!

Aura Lee

Traditional, arranged by Chris Proctor

Accompaniment Patterns

Jim Wood

Many folks probably began picking the same way I did: I plunked around on one of my dad's guitars until I found the G, C, and D chords. Then I learned how to strum a simple accompaniment to songs and basic tunes, and before too long, I picked up on an alternating bass pattern that gave a little shape to the strumming. And eventually, I worked out some walk-ups to chord changes.

In most contexts, basic chord strumming, in one form or another, is enough. But if you add a few standard fingerpicking patterns to your bag of tricks, you can open up new worlds for your rhythm playing. With fingerstyle accompaniment, you can create subtle timbres and textures that suit a large variety of styles and songs. And once you have a couple of the fundamental techniques down, you will find opportunities at every turn.

RIGHT-HAND TECHNIQUES

Adding a few standard fingerpicking patterns to your bag of tricks can open up new worlds for your rhythm playing.

There are a couple of different right-hand methods for fingerstyle accompaniment, and each one has its pros and cons. You can use your ring finger, your middle finger, and a flatpick, which you hold between your thumb and index finger. Or, you can just use your thumb, index, and middle fingers. If you don't use a flatpick, you might want to use some configuration of metal or plastic thumb- and fingerpicks. At any rate, the type of right-hand technique that is best for you depends upon the sound you want, the type of guitar you use, and the circumstances in which you play.

I like to shift between fingerpicking and strumming within the same song—to create different textures for verses and choruses, for example. The most comfortable way for me to achieve this effect is to use a flatpick along with my middle and ring fingers (on which I leave my nails a little longer than usual). People who use the thumb and fingers do have the option of playing more elaborate patterns, however. You must survey your own situation and decide which way to go.

Musical examples in this lesson use *p, m,* and *a* to designate flatpick, middle finger, and ring finger, respectively. You can convert this to thumb, index finger, and middle finger.

Introduction

A BASIC PATTERN

The first picking pattern, which is used in Examples 1 through 5, works well from 72 to 120 beats per minute. Of course, you will probably have to practice this pattern at a slower tempo in order to build up to this speed. Remember that the pick strokes (with the flatpick or thumb) should always go down.

In Examples 2 through 5, this first pattern is adapted slightly to work with four other archetypal chords. Your left hand should hold down the chord, as if you were strumming, while your right hand picks the individual notes within that chord. In addition, the picking sequence should remain the same for each chord even though the string or chord tone (the root, third, or fifth) may be different at any given place in the measure.

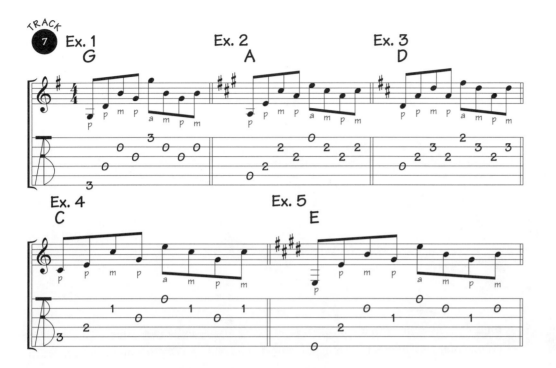

OTHER PATTERNS

The second pattern, shown in Example 6, works similarly to the first pattern but is adapted for the 3/4 meter. The third pattern, used in Example 7, seems to groove best between 80 and 100 beats per minute. The fourth pattern, used in Example 8, can work as slowly as 80 up to as fast as you can handle. And the fifth pattern, used in Example 9, also sounds great around 80. Example 9 sounds half as fast as the preceding two examples because it has an eighth-note feel instead of a 16th-note feel. The sixth pattern, used in Example 10, is the waltz version of Example 9.

WORKING IN CHORD PROGRESSIONS

Now that you have a few basic patterns under your belt, Examples 11–14 show some generic chord progressions that use your new technique. To give you an idea or two, I've included some walk-ups and such along with the basic patterns that I've just shown you. For instance, check out the bass line in Example 11, measures 2 and 6. Measure 8 of Example 11 has a pull-off, and there's a grace note in the first measure of Example 14.

As you can see, these progressions vary from the basic patterns, but the fundamental grooves are the same. By the time you get these examples rolling along, you will, I'm sure, have discovered a hundred ways to integrate fingerstyle accompaniment into your own repertoire.

TRACK 9 Ex. 11

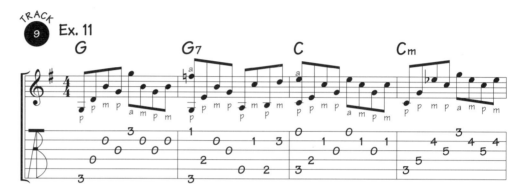

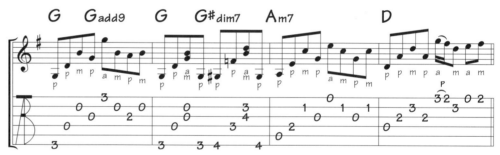

TRACK 10 Ex. 12

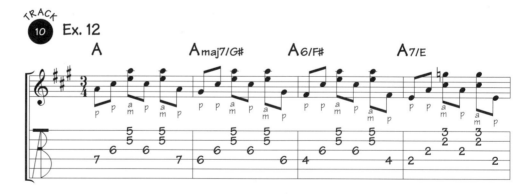

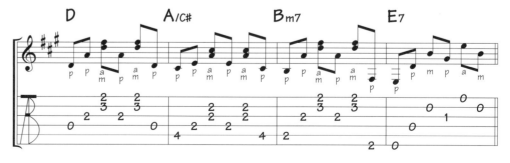

Ex. 13

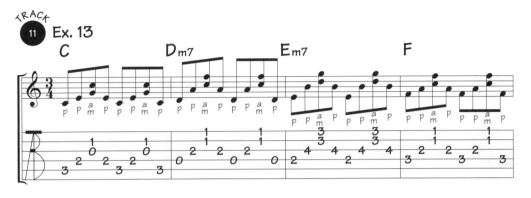

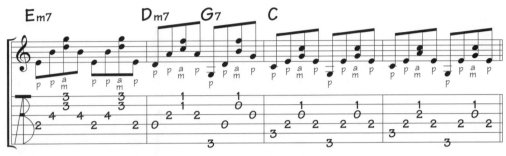

Ex. 14

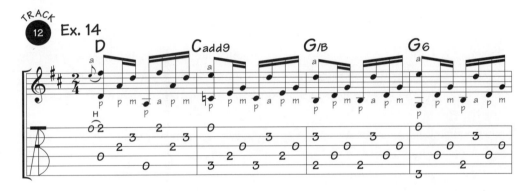

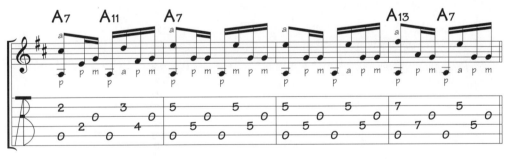

Steady Bass Fingerpicking

David Hamburger

A simple bass drone lets you improvise bluesy licks on top.

Introduction

Playing fingerstyle takes a lot of coordination. The first tunes I learned were basic alternating-thumb or Travis-picking arrangements, and I tended to play them over and over without much variation, just enjoying the fact that I could finally play them right. While it's certainly possible to improvise in the Travis style, as a beginner I was quite pleased when I stumbled across the simpler, bluesier steady-bass approach.

Thumping out a steady bass drone with your thumb lets you spin bluesy, single-note licks over the top with your fingers as an improvised alternative to the folkier-sounding alternating-bass style. The following examples should help you get coordinated in this steady-bass style. With a little work, you'll be able to keep yourself entertained for hours on end.

THUMPING OUT THE BASS

Example 1 is about getting used to the roles your thumb and fingers are going to play. Example 1a gives you the steady bass in quarter notes on the low E string. In 1b, you pinch the high and low strings simultaneously on the downbeat, then continue to carry the bass for the next three beats. In 1c, pinch the high string on the first and third beats, always maintaining the bass with your thumb. In 1d, make the pinches on the first and second beats only, and in 1e on the first and fourth beats.

Example 2 introduces the idea of eighth-note syncopation. Make the first pinch on the downbeat, and then repeat the note—that second note on the high string falls between the first and second beats. Examples 2b through 2e introduce fretted notes on the B string and involve similar eighth-note syncopations throughout each bar. You can practice each of these examples as a continuous loop: keep the steady bass going and just keep playing the one-bar lick on top over and over until it feels comfortable (or until your roommate/spouse/significant other threatens to do mean things to your guitar with a wire cutter if you don't knock it off).

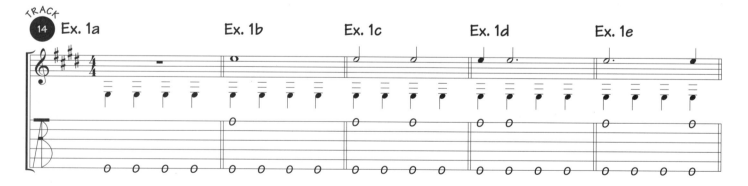

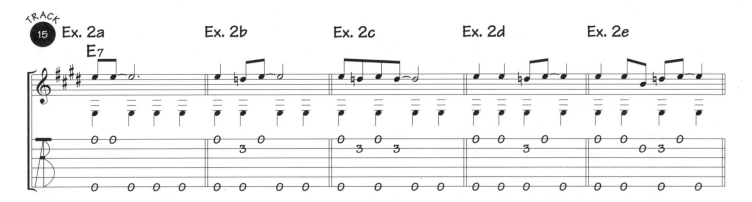

BUILDING BLOCKS OF BLUES

The minor pentatonic scale is one of the fundamental building blocks of blues improvisation. Example 3 illustrates a handful of notes from this scale that you can play without interfering with your bass line. Example 4 is an exercise in playing notes from this scale in an eighth-note pattern and is just one of a zillion possible licks you could work out using this scale.

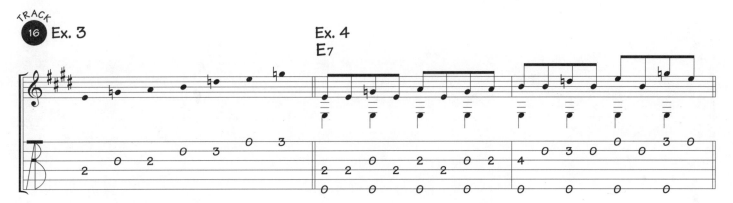

The way you articulate your notes is a big part of the way it sounds and feels to play with this approach. Slides, hammer-ons, and pull-offs all lend a more relaxed and fluid feel to improvising on the guitar, especially in the open position. Example 5 shows three places where sliding into notes in the minor pentatonic scale can be particularly effective. Examples 6 and 7 are licks incorporating one or more of these slides. Example 8 suggests one way to practice hammering on to and pulling off of the same pentatonic notes. The lick in Example 9 is based on combining hammer-ons, pull-offs, and slides.

Since a standard 12-bar blues in E also goes to A7 and B7, let's look at some ways to adapt what we've done so far to those two chords. A slight tweak of the pentatonic scale, replacing D with C♯ on the second string, yields the scale fragment in Example 10. To convey the sound of being on A7, or the IV chord of an E blues, we'll move our thumb up to

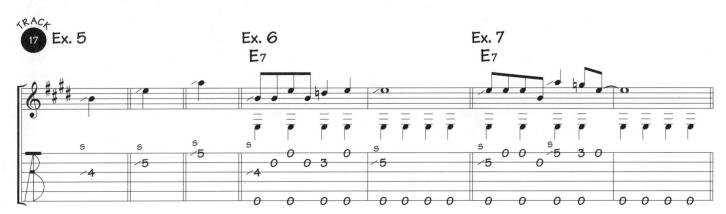

the A string in the bass. Some of the licks we've just done in E work perfectly well in A; all you have to do is move the bass note up to the fifth string. For instance, Example 11 is just Example 9 played over an A bass. Example 12 is the same as Example 6, but with the fifth note of the lick changed from D to C♯ to fit better over an A chord.

SYNCOPATING AND BENDING

Let's get even more syncopated. Example 13 gives you a handful of ways to practice landing eighth notes on the offbeats, the *ands* of *one-and-two-and-three-and-four-and,* all while maintaining a steady bass. Try out these exercises, and then give Example 14 a shot. It's a two-measure lick in A with notes landing on the *and* of beats 1 and 2 in the second measure.

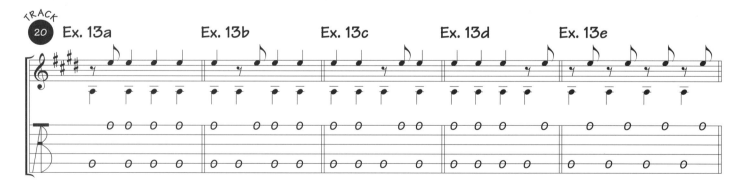

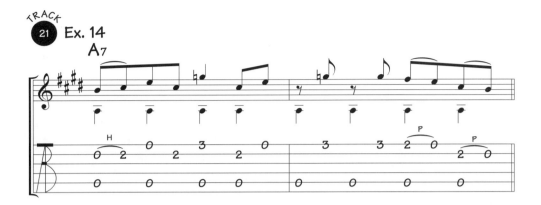

Finally, let's look at what to do over the B7. First of all, you've got to hold down a fretted bass note, the B on the second fret of the fifth string. Then, by changing the G to F♯ in the E-minor pentatonic scale, we get Example 15. Note the recommended left-hand fingerings, which should help you to coordinate your fretboard efforts.

Bending is particularly effective on the B chord; the quarter-tone bend is a standard blues move, and it works well here on the D. You want to push the string to one side, raising the pitch up toward (but not quite reaching) a D♯. Practice this over the steady bass, as in Example 16. Then try incorporating the quarter-tone bend into a rhythmically straightforward lick like Example 17, or something more syncopated, like Example 18. These licks sound perfectly good without the bend as well.

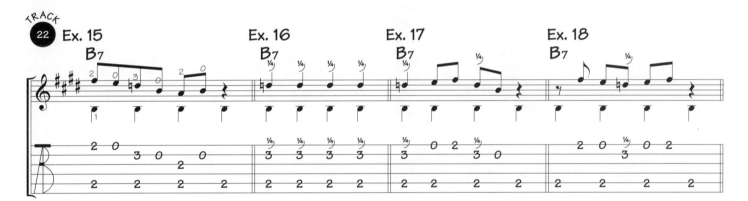

PLAYING A 12-BAR BLUES

Example 19 is a 12-bar blues in E incorporating all of the elements we've worked on so far. The bass is solid quarter notes throughout, shifting from E to A to B to reflect the chords of the standard blues progression, and the melody on top involves slides, hammer-ons, pull-offs, quarter-tone bends, and various syncopations and variations on the minor pentatonic scale. It's great fun to be able to accompany yourself while you improvise, and you'll be the hit of your own private party.

TRACK
23
Ex. 19

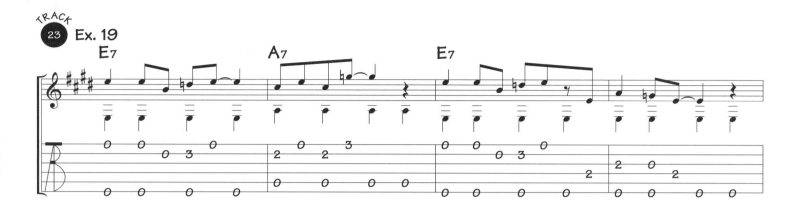

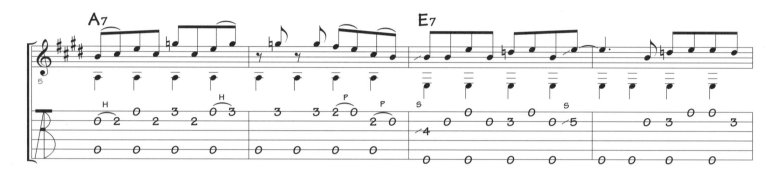

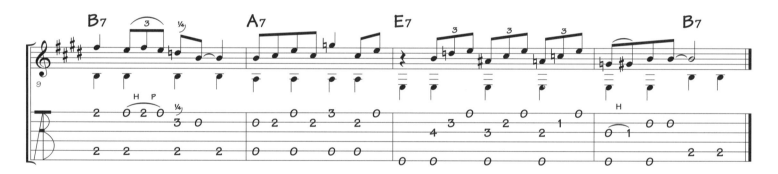

Fingerstyle Improvisation

Dylan Schorer

"Take a solo" is a command that can send most guitarists into an instant panic. You may have watched in awe as a musician improvised one inspired solo after another, or your jaw may have hit the floor the first time you heard a solo guitarist who sounded like two or three people playing at once. If you have little or no experience soloing, or if you can improvise well but have never tried to improvise fingerstyle, it's time to take your first steps toward.

Many people learn to improvise single-string melodies with a pick, but fingerstyle improvisation can be rewarding and is often a better way to begin. Single-string improvisation usually sounds better when you have accompaniment, such as tapes to play along with or a friend who is willing to be your rhythm guitar slave. Fingerpicking allows you to supply your own accompaniment with your thumb while playing the melody with your other fingers, a technique that can make even simple melodies sound good.

You must first learn to think of your fingerstyle playing as two independent parts: bass and melody.

TWO-TRACK MIND

You must first learn to think about your fingerstyle playing as two independent parts—bass and melody. The goal is to be able to keep a steady bass line going with your thumb and play a totally independent melody above that.

For all of the following exercises, we're going to use dropped-D tuning, which provides two open-string D notes. You arrive at dropped-D tuning by lowering the sixth string down a whole step from E to D. Use your fourth string as a reference; the sixth string should sound one octave lower than the fourth.

The best way to begin improvising is to learn scales. Scales are like road maps of your fretboard that tell you which notes sound good in each key.

We'll begin by learning the major scale in the key of D. Your thumb is going to play the bass notes on the bottom three strings, so the melody will be limited to the top three strings and won't be affected by the fact that your guitar is in dropped-D tuning. Here are two versions of the D-major scale in second position.

Introduction TRACK 24

D-major scale

Or

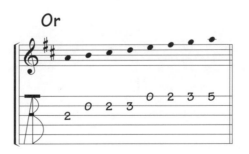

THE RIGHT HAND

Now let's look at the right hand. Practice alternating from the sixth to fourth strings with your thumb (see Example 1). Once you feel comfortable with that, try adding a melody note. In Example 2, your thumb continues to alternate between the fourth and sixth strings, while your middle or index finger plays a melody note on the first beat. The melody note can be any note from the D-major scale, on any of the top three strings. Continue the pattern and play a different melody note from the scale in each measure.

Listen to how each note sounds against the bass line. Some notes create more tension and dissonance than others. The notes in an open D chord sound good against the bass line, especially the third fret, second string, which is a D—the root note of the scale. The root is a good place to begin and end phrases because of its stable, resolved sound.

In Example 3 there are two melody notes per measure. Every time your thumb plays the sixth string you will also play a melody note with your middle or index finger. This more complex pattern allows you to play more interesting melodies.

When you feel comfortable with the pattern in Example 3, try playing four melody notes per measure—one melody note per beat (Example 4). This pattern opens up even more melodic possibilities but tends to sound a bit clunky because the melody just chugs along with the bass line. You therefore wouldn't want to play an entire solo with this pattern, but it can work well for short phrases.

Every melody note we have played so far has been on the downbeat. The next step is to add some syncopation by playing some notes on the upbeat. Syncopation brings fingerstyle playing to life. Example 5 includes a melody note on the first beat and another between the second and third beats. It helps to count the rhythm like this: *1, 2 and 3, 4.* You can also try adding two syncopated notes per measure (Example 6). When playing this pattern, try counting *1, 2 and 3 and 4.*

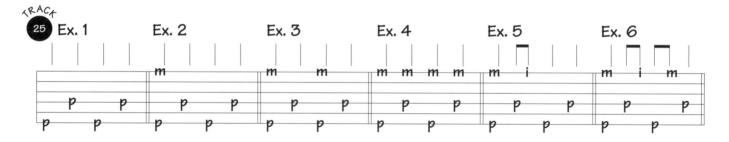

By using all of these patterns and combining notes from the D-major scale, you'll be able to come up with some great-sounding improvisations. You can use this approach to play a break in the middle of a song or to create an intro or an entire song. Example 7 shows what you can do with this technique.

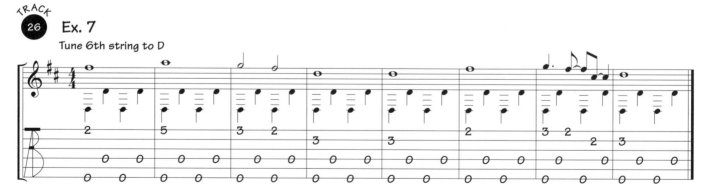

As you first start to improvise, spend a lot of time trying different combinations of notes and playing note combinations with several different picking patterns. Whenever you stumble across a melody you like, write it down or file it in your mental catalogue of licks. As you become familiar with the scale, imagine what each note will sound like before you play it. Part of becoming a good improviser means having a large supply of faithful patterns and melodies and being familiar with the sound of each note in the scale.

You will probably tire pretty quickly of using the same eight melody notes. You can add some new notes to your improvisations by playing the D-major scale in seventh (rather than second) position:

D-major scale

By playing in a different position, you're likely to stumble across new patterns and melodies, and you'll have two places on the neck where you can improvise. You can play a few licks in second position and then slide up to seventh position for a couple of bars, or you can write melodies that move between the two positions.

ADDING CHORDS AND EMBELLISHMENTS

So far, everything we have played has your thumb plodding faithfully between the open D strings, but you could also throw in a few other chords in the key of D, such as G and A. You need to play only the bass notes to imply a particular chord. For example, you could imply a G chord by alternating your thumb between the sixth and fourth strings, with your left hand fingering the sixth string at the fifth fret, or you could imply an A chord by alternating between the open fifth string and the fourth string fretted at the second fret. But remember that with your left hand fretting the bass notes of a chord, the melody will be limited to the notes you can reach from that position.

Another way to make your melodies more interesting is to use hammer-ons, pull-offs, and slides. You can also try throwing in some double-stops—playing two notes together in the melody. Check out Example 8 for a sample of how all of these techniques can fall together into a solo.

As you become more comfortable with these techniques, you will eventually feel like your thumb is on auto-pilot, and you'll be free to play anything you like over your own accompaniment. Soon you'll be on the receiving end of those awed looks.

Whenever you stumble across a melody you like, write it down or file it away in your mind.

Ex. 8

Tune 6th string to D

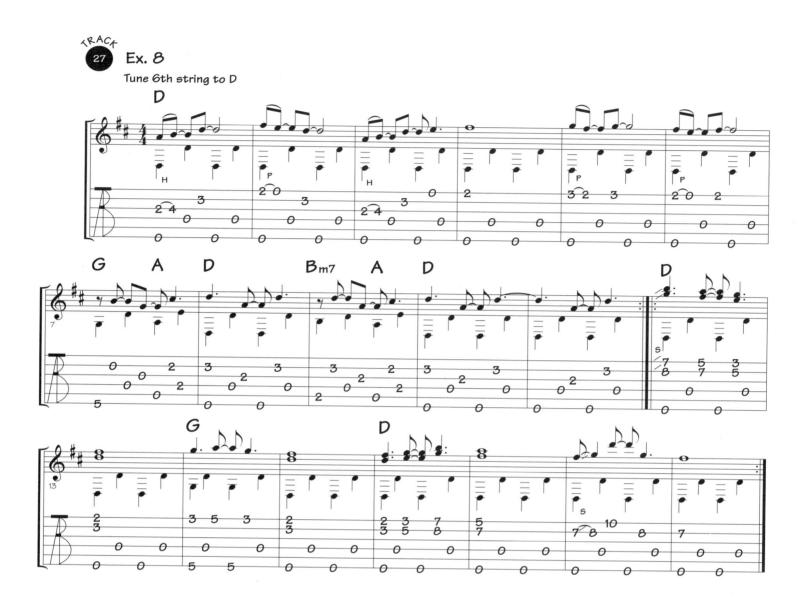

Melodies and Bass Lines

David Hamburger

'm all for the Delta blues, with its thumpy drone on the tonic, and much of my adolescence was happily misspent in pursuit of the stride piano–inspired boom-chick of Travis picking. But the first time I saw someone sitting alone at a piano, churning out a steady 4/4 bass line with his left hand while his right hand splashed blues licks up and down the keyboard, I was transfixed. Also jealous. There's nothing groovier than a walking bass line. The simple solution seemed to be to become a pianist, which I spent all of four months trying to do. I was ultimately overwhelmed, however, by the prospect of getting my two hands to do two completely different things at the same time.

Abandoning my hopes of becoming the next Oscar Peterson, I still found myself faced with the original dilemma: how to play that spellbinding combination of walking bass lines and blues licks simultaneously. I concluded that I'd just have to find a way to do it on the guitar.

This two-part lesson is the hard-won results of my penetrating and exhaustive research into the matter. My approach generally adhered to the following rigorous and highly academic (ahem) methodology.

1. Familiarize yourself with the literature. In my case, this included wearing out copies of Stefan Grossman and John Renbourn's *Under the Volcano* and *Stefan Grossman and John Renbourn,* two out-of-print LPs that have been loosely compiled onto the CD *Snap a Little Owl* (Shanachie). I also squandered valuable homework time attempting to pick apart Joe Pass' work on his duet albums with Ella Fitzgerald, particularly *Fitzgerald and Pass . . . Again,* which are available from Pablo/Fantasy. See if you can track them down or try to find the Joe Pass/Herb Ellis guitar duets on the Concord label.

2. Obtain a working understanding of what bass lines are and how they work in the blues. I quickly discovered that the best bass lines are played by bass players. B.B. King's *Live at the Regal* (MCA) and the Allman Brothers' *Live at the Fillmore East* (Polydor), two albums from which I had previously lifted only guitar licks, each featured a whole band of outstanding musicians, including the great bassists Leo Lauchie and Berry Oakley, respectively.

3. Work out some of these bass lines on the guitar, while simultaneously playing simple chords or blues phrases on the high strings. It helps to start off in guitar-friendly keys, such as E and A. It also helps to work out combinations of bass lines and chords in one-bar units, much like learning a Travis-picking pattern one bar at a time: here's what to play on an E chord, here's a lick that works over an A7, etc.

4. Practice the resulting combinations. I chose to do so in front of reruns of *Gilligan's Island* with the sound turned down. My working theory was that witnessing the noble efforts of the passengers and crew of the SS *Minnow* to impose order and civilization on the hostile and uncaring tropical isle they were forced to call home might inspire me in my own struggle to impose a contrapuntal, pianistic sense of the blues on the harsh and unforgiving fretboard of the instrument I have come to love in spite of myself.

There's nothing groovier than a walking bass line, especially when played simultaneously with blues licks.

Introduction

So with these high standards and hints in mind, let's get rolling. In Part I, we'll look at maintaining chords in the treble register while learning some standard bass lines; in Part II, we'll move into playing single-note and double-stop riffs over bass lines.

PART I
ISOLATING THE BASS LINE

In the beginning, it will help if your fretting hand has only one thing to concentrate on. Try playing Example 1a. The bass line requires your left hand; the top notes do not. The thumb of your picking hand plays the descending bass line, the notes that are stem-down in the notation. At the same time, your right index and middle fingers or middle and ring fingers keep the top part of an E chord—shown stem-up—ringing through the measure. Example 1b has the same chord tones on top, over an ascending bass line.

It helps to work out combinations of bass lines and chords in one-bar units.

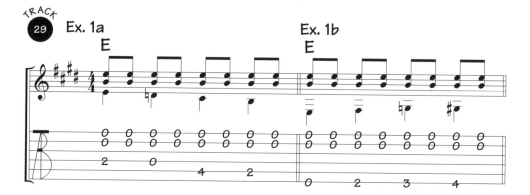

Example 2 takes a similar approach to an A7 chord. Again, the bass line requires fretting, while the two open strings are used for the top notes. Try picking the G string with your index finger, the high E with your ring finger, and, of course, the bass line with your thumb. Also experiment with different fingerings to see what's comfortable. Example 2b is the same as 2a, but with an ascending bass line.

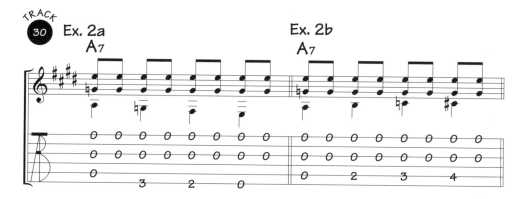

It gets a little trickier when you have to hold down fretted notes on top. Part of the solution to this problem lies in being flexible and creative with your fretting-hand fingerings. Try playing the E7 pattern in Example 3a, holding down the third fret on the B string with your middle finger while your ring and index fingers handle the bass line. In Example 3b, add your pinky at the fourth fret on the G string and keep playing the bass notes with your index finger at the second fret and your ring finger at the fourth fret.

A nearly identical fingering will get you through a similar set of moves over an A7, as shown in Example 4.

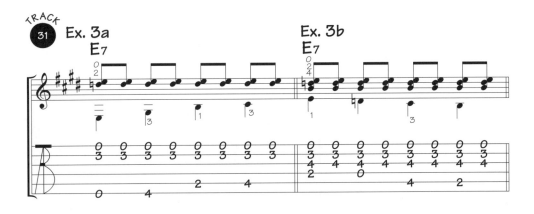

ADDING NOTES

So far, each of these examples has maintained a steady flow of eighth notes on top, played against a bass line of steady quarter notes. Example 5a implies the 12/8 feel of a slow blues by placing triplets over a quarter-note bass line. Blues and jazz bass players will frequently play twice as many notes to the bar on a slow blues by repeating every note of the bass line, as shown in Example 5b. You can think of this doubled-up bass line the way it's expressed in the notation—as pairs of notes played on the first and third beats of each set of triplets.

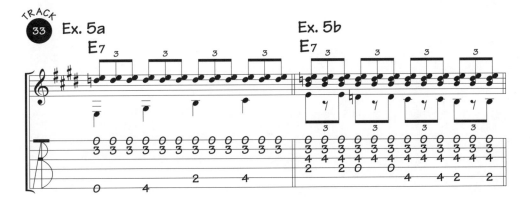

In Example 6, you're not grabbing all the notes of a chord simultaneously with your picking hand, but breaking them up into an arpeggio. Using your ring finger for the high string, your middle finger for the second string, and your index finger for the third string, roll back through the A7 chord on top while maintaining the descending, doubled-up bass line underneath.

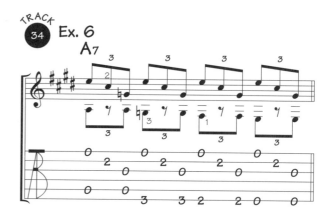

Examples 7 and 8 illustrate two different ways to harmonize the bass line. In Example 7a, notes on the G string are used to harmonize the bass line in the key of E. Notice that the bass line is in eighth notes while the treble is simply in quarter notes. In Example 7b, the high E string is used as a common tone against the same harmonized line, with the same combination of quarter and eighth notes. As in Example 2, try using your index finger to pick the third string and your ring finger to pick the high E string. Example 8a is a similar harmony in the key of A. In Example 8b, the open G string functions as a common tone throughout the measure: G♮ is the flatted seventh of an A7 chord.

WALKING IN B

Of course, if you're dealing with E and A chords, it would be good to have a few ideas for handling B7 chords as well. You would then be able to walk through the I (E), IV (A), and V (B7) of a 12-bar blues in E using bass line and chord combinations throughout the entire chord progression.

In Example 9, use your index, middle, and ring fingers to pick the top three strings, while your thumb spells out the descending bass line. Example 10a is based on the same idea, but with triplet phrasing on the top. Example 10b has the doubled-bass sound underneath a triplet arpeggiation of the B7 chord.

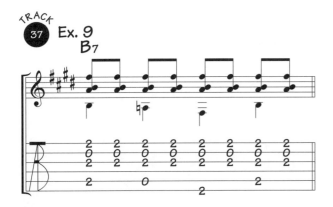

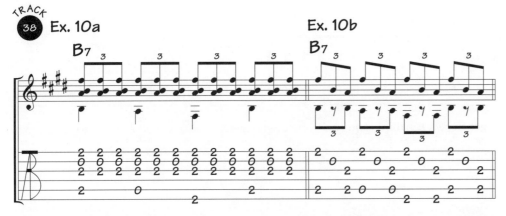

Example 11a is a simple harmonization in tenths of an ascending bass line in B, while Example 11b is a more jazz-inflected, chordal style of harmonization.

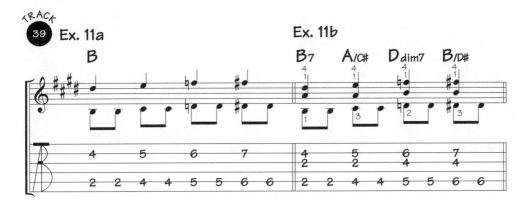

Since the whole idea behind learning these examples is playing the blues, I've provided a 12-bar blues in E in Example 12, with a walking bass line that goes from start to finish. The entire progression follows a standard I–IV–V pattern, but it can be broken down into one-bar phrases similar to the ones found in Examples 1 through 11, with a few slight variations. Specifically, in measure 11 of Example 12, the fourth quarter note of the bass line is a C♮, not a B as in Example 1a. The C in this case is a chromatic passing tone—a note that leads you by half steps from one note to another, in this case from C♯ to B. By playing C♮ on the fourth beat of measure 11, you are setting up the B on the downbeat of measure 12, rather than just repeating the same note (B) for two beats in a row. Also note that measure 7 is a variation on Example 7b that breaks the chord tones on top into triplets rather than grabbing them simultaneously as quarter notes.

Finally, watch out for the triplets that appear on the third beat of measures 11 and 12, which break up the otherwise steady flow of eighth notes.

Try to familiarize yourself with these various moves. In Part II we'll look at playing riffs over bass lines and learn how to handle turnarounds.

TRACK 40 Ex. 12

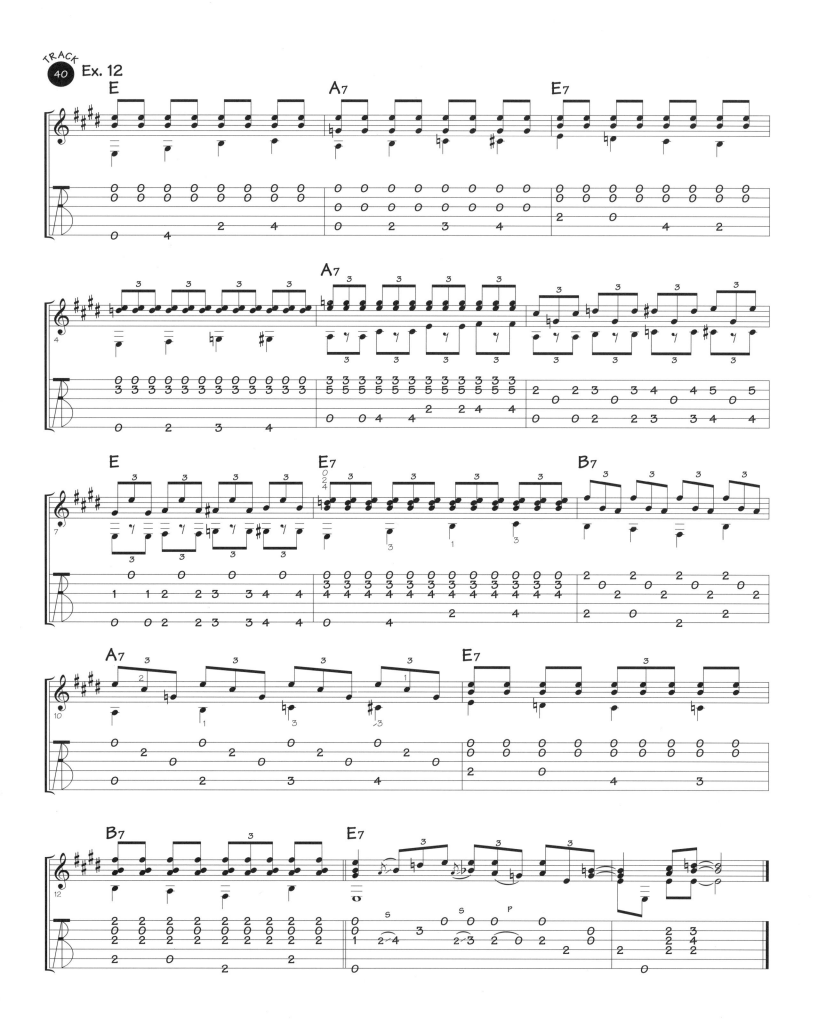

PART II

We've looked at the basic mechanics of playing double-stops and chords over a steady walking bass line, using the I, IV, and V chords in the key of E: E7, A7, and B7. This is a good way of developing independence between the fingers and thumb of your picking hand, and it can lead your fretting hand into some new and challenging territory as well.

Now we'll take this idea a step further and learn how to play melodic lines over a walking bass line. We'll combine the bass lines from Part I with some simple single-note and double-stop riffs and work our way up to more elaborate melodic ideas.

Keep in mind that we're dealing with two horizontal ideas: a melody lick and a bass line. That's what's going on musically, and that's ultimately what you want to appreciate, understand, and convey: bass and melody moving forward simultaneously. The execution of that sound, however, is basically a series of vertical technical challenges; you are constantly trying to do two things at once. As we go through these examples, try to break them down beat by beat and see what they demand of your fingers at each moment. Then you can begin to deal with where you came from in the last beat and where you are going in the next beat.

This walking bass/melody approach affords some satisfying turnaround ideas.

A BASIC BLUES LICK

Introduction   TRACK 41

Example 1a is a basic blues lick over an E bass line. Try playing just the lick on the high E string before combining it with the bass line. Then, as you begin to work out the lick with the bass line, work through the measure beat by beat. In beat 1, pinch the open string on the bottom and the third fret on the high string, and then play the open high string. In beat 2, pinch the low and the high string again, this time fretting both at the second fret. That uses just two fingers, and while it's a bit of a stretch, it's easier than playing some of the three- and four-finger chords you already know. Next, play the open high E string again, then the low E string at the third fret for beat 3, and the low E string at the fourth fret for beat 4. Piece of cake!

Example 1b has the same lick on top, with the bass line transposed to A. Take the same step-by-step approach we used to get a handle on Example 1a.

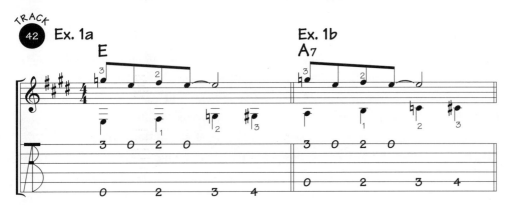

EXPANDING THE PHRASE

Example 2 expands on the basic melodic phrase used in Example 1. In Example 2a, the bass line is the same as in Example 1a. The first four notes in the melody are the same too, but now the phrase is carried over into the second half of the measure. First just play the melody lick to get the timing of the tied notes, the triplets, and the hammer-on to the second fret of the B string in beat 4. The ties accent the offbeats, which may seem harder to play at first. However, if we take the same blow-by-blow approach, it can actually be a little easier to play these kinds of phrases than to always be pinching bass and melody together on the downbeat.

The first half of Example 2a is the same as the first half of 1a, so let's pick it up in the middle of the bar, on beat 3. The high open E picked at the end of beat 2 is still ringing out, so you don't have to hit it again. You've just got to play the third fret on the low E string with your thumb on the downbeat, the same as in Example 1a, and then follow that up with the open B string. Not a problem. Beat 4 is a little tricky. You've got to pick the low string with your thumb while simultaneously hammering on to the second fret of the B string. After you've made this heroic maneuver, all it takes to finish up the measure is hitting the open high E string and the second-fret B string, which you've been holding down since you hammered on to it. Example 2b is the same thing over an A bass line.

Example 3a brings us more melody notes on the offbeats, with a new bass line. The direction of the melody lick is reversed in Example 3b to fit better over an A chord (it's ♭3, 3, root over the E chord; and ♭7, 6, 5 over the A chord). In both of these examples, the syncopation of the melody means you have to do less simultaneous pinching of two notes and more pick-a-bass-note/pick-a-melody-note, almost like Travis picking.

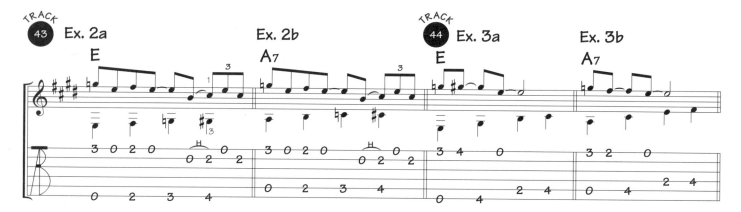

HARMONIZING THE MELODY

In Part I, we played some licks that involved harmonizing the bass line. Example 4 shows how you can take the licks from Example 3, keep the same bass line going, and harmonize the melody line. Example 4a is the harmonized version of Example 3a. Use the index and ring fingers of your picking hand to get the first two pairs of notes on the first and third strings, while your thumb plays the bass notes as usual. Use your middle and ring fingers to grab the third pair of notes on top: the open second and first strings. In Example 4b, the harmonized version of Example 3b, it helps to use a half barre to fret the second pair of notes in the melody: the second fret of the first and third strings.

Example 5 makes use of a descending bass line, and the melody is a sort of harmonization of that bass line; for the first two beats of the measure, the melody note on the downbeat is a tenth above the bass note. In Example 5a (as in Example 1a), the use of open notes in the melody and the bass line means you rarely have to fret more than one note at a time. Example 5b has a bit more going on in the fingering department but still never more than two fretted notes at a time.

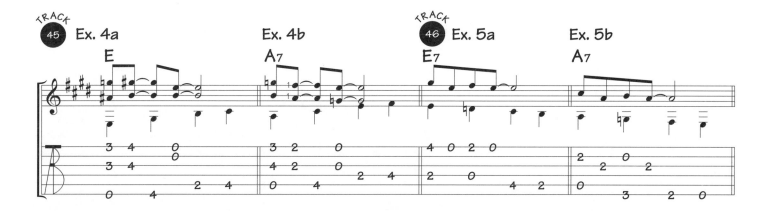

VARYING THE BASS LINE

Examples 6a and 6b introduce a new kind of bass line. It's akin to the doubled-up bass lines we used for the shuffle feel in Part I, but this time we're sticking with just quarter notes. What's new is that we're perched halfway between a simple drone on the tonic and the kind of full-fledged walking bass lines we've used so far, where every beat is a new note. This is another idea used by jazz bassists, who often employ it to create a little breathing room. In our case, any of the other bass lines we've used until now would clash harmonically with the double-stops on top, because unlike most of the single-note phrases we've played thus far, these double-stop licks outline the harmony of the chord explicitly. The fingerings indicated in the notation should help you grab these two licks.

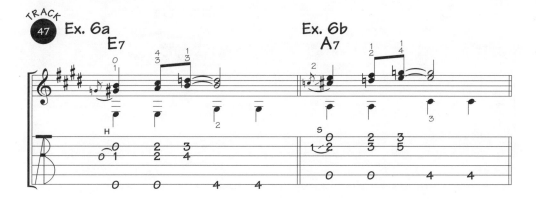

Now let's tackle the B7 chord. Despite the lack of an open B note in the bass, walking bass licks in B are greatly aided by the presence of an open B melody note (played on the second string) and both ♭7 and ♭3 notes in the bass—the open A and D strings, which give your fretting hand a bit of a break.

Remember the basic approach. Play the melody and the bass line separately to hear and feel them individually. Then break down the bass-and-melody relationship beat by beat. In Example 7, make sure the quarter-tone bend is heard going up only; block the B string with your picking finger as you release the bend, and then keep that finger on the string, ready to pick the open B string next.

Example 8 begins with a four-digit pinch. Use your index, middle, and ring fingers for the third, second, and first strings, respectively, as your thumb grabs the bass note. Your left hand has to change positions in a pretty big way on the second beat. You can begin to make the switch during that open high E string right after the four-note chord, but try not to cut off the chord too soon. After that, the remainder of the bar is pretty easy to play. Example 9 goes places you wouldn't ordinarily expect to go from an open B7, and yet the open strings make it work.

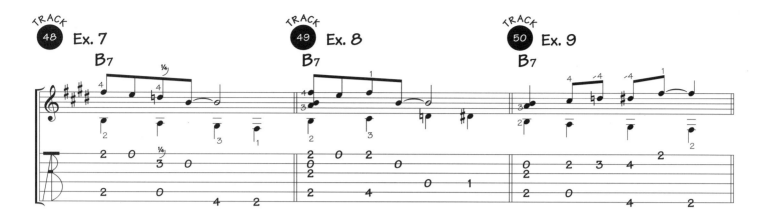

TURNAROUNDS

For some reason, turnarounds hold a special place in the hearts of guitar players, up there with favorite old LPs, first good guitars, and the dream of being able to afford roadies someday. This walking bass/melody approach is well suited to coming up with some satisfying turnaround ideas. The first turnaround I ever uncovered in this style just came from taking a standard bass-line walk-up from I to V and a standard melodic turnaround lick and seeing what happened when I tried to play them at the same time, as shown in Example 10.

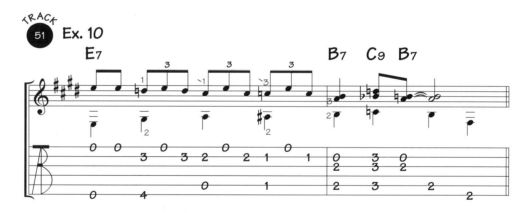

You might often discover that the two voices, bass and treble, suggest the sound of a fuller chord. Example 11 shows one way of taking Example 10 and filling in the middle voice, with some interesting chordal results.

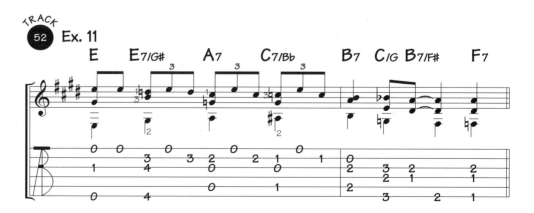

Example 12 shows what's possible if you stretch this idea a little further. It combines the same bass-line walkup to V found in the previous examples with a position-jumping blues lick that begins with the classic country blues double-stop quarter-tone bend up from the ♭3 of E and has a Buddy Guy–style ♭5 hammer-on held against the root double-stop thrown in for good measure. Finally, Example 13 combines an essentially descending bass line from I to V with another triplet-laden blues lick that rolls through the ♭VI chord (C9) before landing on the V (B).

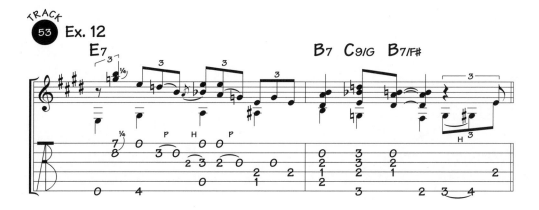

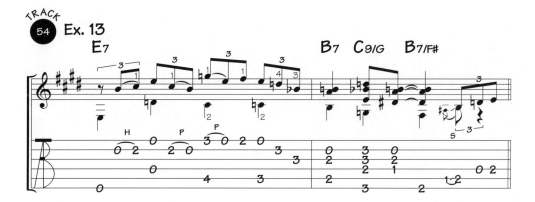

PUTTING IT ALL TOGETHER

Now, as the hipsters say, let's play the blues. Example 14 is a 12-bar blues in E. Like Part I's chordal example, it's meant to hang together as a complete piece of music, although each bar is simply a one-measure bass line/melody unit like the ones we've been working on. The turnaround is a perfect example of the kind of blues counterpoint that can sound all wrong until you get it up to tempo. Each line makes sense on its own (again, practice them separately at first), but there are some heavy dissonances involved when you play them together—in particular, the A♮ in the melody against the G♯ bass note on the second beat of measure 11. Don't worry if it sounds weird when you isolate this move for practice; at tempo, you'll hear the two separate lines passing through this moment, each with enough melodic integrity to remain convincing.

Banjo Technique for Guitar

Dick Weissman

The unique sound we associate with the banjo is due in large part to a variety of right-hand techniques that banjo players typically use. Many of these techniques can be adapted for the guitar to provide some interesting variations on traditional guitar sounds.

A number of guitar players have explored these ideas in their work. Richie Havens, for example, uses flatpicking strums characteristic of the tenor banjo technique heard in music of the 1920s. Bluegrass banjo rolls have been transformed into guitar cross-picking by players such as Doc Watson, Clarence White, and Dan Crary. Tommy Flint is one of many guitarists who have applied melodic banjo style (also known as chromatic style) to the guitar.

One of the most familiar banjo techniques is frailing, also referred to as clawhammer, down-picking, or rapping. Jody Stecher and Martin Simpson have both adapted this technique to the guitar to great effect. The musical examples in this lesson will introduce you to frailing on the guitar.

Down-picking is perhaps the most appropriate term for this technique, which is based on picking down on the strings with your fingernails. The basic pattern used on the banjo involves picking down on a single string with the back of either your index or middle fingernail, brushing down across two or three strings with the back of the fingernail, and then plucking the fifth string with your thumb. The rhythm is a quarter note followed by two eighth notes.

You can play the first note of the strum with your index or middle finger. I use my index finger because its nail is much stronger than the nail on my middle finger, and it is virtually impossible to down-pick without using the nail. I find that metal fingerpicks make too much noise. I have experimented with the plastic aLaska Pik, which is worn on the finger like a ring. In any case, the choice is yours. I have known many fine banjo players, including Art Rosenbaum, who prefer to use the middle finger for picking the first note of the strum.

The fifth string is the highest open string on the five-string banjo. When frailing the guitar, try singling out a specific bass string for the third step in the pattern. The string you choose to pluck will depend on the key of the particular piece you're playing. In the key of A, you might want to use the open fifth string or you might choose to alternate between the open fifth string and the open sixth string.

Banjo frailing can be adapted to the guitar to great effect.

Introduction TRACK 56

FRAILING EXERCISES

Example 1 alternates between a D and a C chord and is intended to teach you to play individual strings with the back of your fingernail with some degree of accuracy. In Example 2, you will be executing the basic frailing strum, which includes individual notes and a bass drone. With the D chord, play the drone on the open fourth string; and with the C chord, finger it at the fourth string, second fret (an E note).

Although frailing is quite useful on the guitar in regular tuning, it is much more dramatic when you retune the guitar to highlight the use of the low drone string. Tune your sixth string down to a D note and play the passage in Example 3. This musical example involves picking individual strings and occasionally strumming a D chord.

In standard tuning, modify your strum to include hammering on a note with your left hand. In Example 4, finger a C chord, but take your middle finger off the fourth string to play it open. Pick down on the open fourth string; hammer-on at the fourth string, second fret, with your left-hand middle finger; brush down across the first, second, and third strings; and, finally, play the fifth string at the third fret with your thumb. The rhythm is four even eighth notes (hence, two of these patterns are in this 4/4 measure).

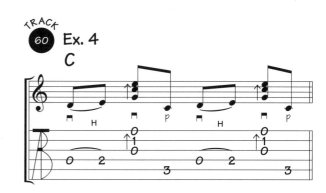

Example 5 requires you to tune your third string to a high G, like the octave third string on a 12-string guitar. In order to avoid breaking the string, you'll need to use a very light gauge, such as a .009. Your third string is now tuned exactly like the fifth string of a banjo, which will enable you to simulate banjo and dulcimer effects. Notice that in this example the rhythm of the frailing is broken up (there are very few strums).

"OLD JOE CLARK"

The version of "Old Joe Clark" shown on the next page, which is based on the second part of that tune, utilizes most of the frailing techniques we've discussed thus far. It is arranged in dropped-D tuning. All the single melody notes are frailed with the back of the first or second fingernail, and the bass drone notes are played with the thumb.

Other modifications to this basic clawhammer pattern can help you keep things interesting. You can rework the sequence of the right-hand fingers so that the thumb leads, or start the pattern by strumming a chord. It is also possible to combine up-picking and down-picking to achieve further variations of sound and texture.

Remember that the most common tuning of the five-string banjo (G D G B D) is almost identical to open-G tuning on the guitar (D G D G B D), and that open G and other open tunings are particularly effective with frailing. So tune those strings down and see what Uncle Dave Macon or Ralph Stanley might sound like playing your guitar!

Old Joe Clark

Traditional, arranged by Dick Weissman

Arranging Basics

Mark Hanson

When I was working on my music degree years ago, I came across an idea about composing from the great Russian-American composer Igor Stravinsky. Before he started writing a new piece, he would define his parameters: style, harmony, form, instrumentation, and the like. Then he would embark on the actual composition of notes and assigning of instrumentation. The solo guitar idiom does not present the immensity of challenges that writing for a full orchestra does, but when composing or arranging a new guitar instrumental, guitarists can do much worse than to follow Stravinsky's lead.

After learning how to arrange, you may very well start coming up with your own melodies and your own compositions.

In the first of this lesson's two parts, we'll focus on the "rules" of arranging for solo guitar, ending with an arrangement of "How Can I Keep from Singing?" In Part II, we'll focus on breaking the rules. I'll walk you through my arrangement of "If I Only Had a Brain," Harold Arlen's classic tune from *The Wizard of Oz*.

After learning how to arrange, you may very well start coming up with your own melodies.

PART I
SETTING PARAMETERS

The parameters I set for easy solo guitar arrangements vary with each piece, and they often change drastically as I work on an arrangement. But in general, I apply the following rules to all of my arrangements.

1. Use standard tuning. Unless you're going for a specific sound that requires an altered tuning (for example, D A D G A D for a Celtic piece, open G or open D for a slide tune, etc.), use standard tuning. You're probably most familiar with standard tuning, and it provides a consistent foundation from which to start. If, however, the arrangement develops in such a way that it will be more playable or will sound better in an alternate tuning, go ahead and spin those tuning machines.

Introduction
TRACK 63

2. Make it easy to play. This is a relative decision, of course, since your technical ability will determine whether the arrangement is easy or not. But the easier the piece, the more likely that you'll be able to play it flawlessly.

3. Stay down the neck. The melody should fall on the three treble strings and should not move beyond the third or fourth fret. (Melodies that have a range of more than an octave will require you to stretch this rule.) I often arrange a piece with increasing degrees of difficulty in each verse, using the entire neck in later verses, but for this lesson we'll stay in first position.

4. Stick to one of the easier guitar keys. C, A, G, E, and D are good choices if the tune requires a major key, and Am, Em, and Dm work well for minor keys. This parameter will allow you to use the open strings liberally. If you're arranging a jazz piece, this parameter becomes less important, because jazz is often played in flat keys to accommodate horn players.

5. Take your cues from the original version of the tune. I base my initial harmonization on the original. Then I make chord substitutions and add key changes as my ear and imagination dictate.

Let's apply these parameters to arranging a beautiful song from the Quaker tradition entitled "How Can I Keep from Singing?" This tune has been recorded in a number of places, but my introduction to it was through the Catholic church folk hymnal called *Glory and Praise.*

DETERMINING THE KEY

After you've chosen a tune to arrange, you must determine which key will place the melody on the three treble strings without moving out of first position. This is an exercise in solfège, or ear training. Can you tell which note of the *do-re-mi* scale the melody starts on? Which one it ends on? By training your ear, you will be able to. This ability is exceedingly helpful in making quick decisions when arranging.

To figure out the melodic range of "How Can I Keep from Singing?" sing the first phrase as it is shown in Example 1: *My life flows on.* Notice that the notes of this phrase are identical to the opening phrase of a somewhat more prevalent traditional tune, "The Water Is Wide."

Can you hear that the first two notes of the melody in Example 1—*My life*—are *sol* and *do* from the *do-re-mi* scale? Many melodies start with an ascending *sol-do* movement like this, including "The Water Is Wide," "Here Comes the Bride," "Columbia, the Gem of the Ocean," and "Oh, Shenandoah."

You can also sing the complete *do-re-mi* scale, and then sing the first notes of the tune. Compare the two. Can you determine on which note the melody starts, and when it arrives on *do*? This takes some practice, but you can develop this ability if you work at it.

Ex. 1

MY LIFE FLOWS ON

Deciphering the range of a melody by ear in this manner can be difficult at first. With that in mind, the lesson sidebar "Suggested Keys" provides a list of well-known tunes along with their melodic ranges and suggested keys for fingerstyle solo arrangements.

SUGGESTED KEYS

Here is a list of well-known tunes and suggested user-friendly keys for arranging them. In a number of these tunes, the melodies will span more than one octave, but finding the "out-of-bounds" melody notes shouldn't be difficult.

Amazing Grace
C (*sol* to *sol*)

Blowin' in the Wind
G (*ti* up to *la*)

The Boxer
G (*do* to *do* in verse)

Do-Re-Mi
G (*do* to *do*)

I Got Rhythm
C (*sol* to *sol*)

Ob-La-Di, Ob-La-Da
G (*ti* up an octave to *do*)

Oh, Susanna
A or G (*do* up to *la*)

Proud Mary
C or D (*la* up to *mi*)

This Land Is Your Land
C or D (*sol* up to *fa*)

You've Got a Friend
Em/G (*mi* to *mi* in Em)

Back to "How Can I Keep from Singing?" Now that you know the word *life* in the first phrase is *do,* you should be able to figure out the other notes as well. The word *flows* is *re,* and *on* is *mi.* When you get to the phrase *above earth's lamentations* in Example 2, the syllable *lam* is *sol.* If you can't determine that, sing *do re mi fa sol* and substitute the syllable *lam* for *sol.*

Sing through the rest of the tune as shown in Example 2, and you will find that the syllable *lam* is the highest pitched note in the melody. The first word, *my,* is the lowest-pitched note. So the melodic range of "How Can I Keep from Singing?" is *sol* to *sol.*

Now compare this to the chart of melodic ranges in Example 3. You will find that "How Can I Keep from Singing?" fits beautifully in the key of C, using our parameters of playing in the first position with the melody on the three treble strings. (If a melody ranged from *do* to *do*—"Joy to the World," for instance—the key of G would be the correct one to choose for an easy arrangement.) Example 4 shows you the key-of-C scale notes on the first three frets of the three treble strings.

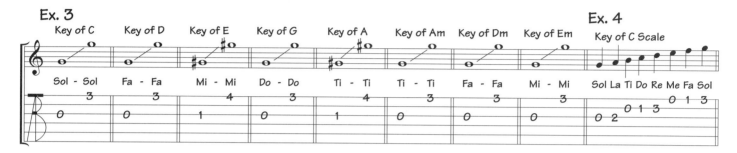

THE CHORDS

Let's return to Example 2, this time paying attention to the chord names above the notes. At this point you need to determine how you're going to alter your chord fingerings to accommodate the melody notes. Often in this style, you will be required to add or subtract a finger from a chord to fret a melody note as it occurs. For example, measure 3 includes an F6/A chord, which adds the little finger to an F chord (on the third fret of the second string). Immediately after that, the little finger lifts to produce the next melody note. This movement happens in measures 11, 19, 20, and 27 as well.

Several other chord alterations occur in this piece. In measure 14, you leave the three treble strings open on a G chord (G6), immediately followed by a D note—second string, third fret. In measure 15, add your little finger again on the D—second string, third fret. This produces a Cadd9 chord. You play that same D note again in measure 22 during an Am chord. In measure 23, fret the first string at the third fret on the Em.

To get your fretting hand going with these alterations, strum the chord on the first beat of each measure and then pick out only the melody notes for the remaining beats of the measure. Try to sustain the bass notes of your chords as much as possible as you fret the melody notes.

THE RHYTHM

Next you need to determine what kind of rhythm and picking sequence you are going to use to accompany the melody. Here are several questions to ask yourself. Will arpeggios work? Will the alternating-bass style provide the proper rhythmic feel? Will scales work as rhythmic fillers, or should I use a combination of scales and arpeggios? Is a chordal pinch on the first beat followed by single melody notes in the rest of the measure enough to carry the arrangement? How about pinches on the first and third beats? Ask yourself some basic questions about the feel of the tune, too. Is it fast or slow? Is the rhythm smooth and flowing or percussive?

THE FULL ARRANGEMENT

In Example 5, I have written out a nice, intermediate-level arrangement of "How Can I Keep from Singing?" in the key of C. The first time through (measures 1–32), play the tune relatively slowly, with a free expansion and contraction of the tempo—a technique called rubato. The second time through, the rhythm changes substantially through the use of a steady alternating-bass pattern. This gives the arrangement an upbeat feel, providing considerable contrast to the first half.

Notice what I have done rhythmically during the long melodic pauses in measures 7–8 and 23–24. I have connected an ascending scale in the bass to an ascending arpeggio on a G chord. To keep this moving line out of the way of the melody, I have arranged it on bass strings that are pitched lower than the previous and upcoming melody notes. This maintains the listeners' interest during the melodic pause without detracting from the melody. Make sure you play this rhythmic filler more quietly than the surrounding melodic phrases!

In measures 17–19, I incorporated an ascending bass line under the melody. This is designed to keep the arrangement from becoming static. Measures 17–18 also use a harmonically strong technique called contrary motion, where two voices—in this case, the ascending bass line and the descending melody line—move in opposite directions.

In measure 11 and several other places in the arrangement you'll find an F chord with the sixth string fretted at the first fret. If both a barre F and an F with the thumb fretting the bass string are beyond your ability, substitute the F/A chord found in measure 3.

ARRANGE YOUR OWN

When arranging pieces, make sure you maintain their musical essence. Be aware of voice leading (the movement of an inner-voice note from one chord to the inner-voice note of the next chord, for example), which provides an interesting line that supports the melody while leaving the important notes of the chord in place. This takes study, understanding, and a keen ear.

How Can I Keep from Singing?

Traditional, arranged by Mark Hanson

PART II

"IF I ONLY HAD A BRAIN"

Fingerstyle guitar solos are a lot like piano solos in that most of them have the melody in the treble, a midrange harmony, and a bass line. This presents myriad technical challenges for guitarists, and working around these challenges is the essence of fingerstyle arranging. Successful guitar arrangements not only sound good but are playable as well.

As I mentioned in Part I, I use some basic parameters for every fingerstyle guitar piece I arrange. I make sure that it's reasonably easy to play; that it's in a "guitar-friendly" key, such as C, A, G, E, D, Am, Em, or Dm; that it's in standard tuning; and that the melody is on the three treble strings and goes no higher than the third or fourth fret.

Of course, rules like these are made to be broken. Let me walk you through my arrangement of "If I Only Had a Brain," Harold Arlen's classic tune from *The Wizard of Oz,* and show you what fun it is to break the rules.

SIMPLICITY IS THE KEY

My arrangement of this tune began with a request from a guitar student who was struggling to make music out of Earl Klugh's beautiful arrangement in the key of D. I tried to create an arrangement that would maintain all of the richness of the original music but would be manageable for intermediate players. I first thought about the range of the melody and what key might make it the most playable. Singing through the melody, I discerned that the lowest note was *sol,* the fifth note of a major scale, and the highest note was *ti,* the seventh note of a major scale. The range is a full octave and a third.

Thus the melody already breaks one of our parameters. It will have to either move above the third fret on the first string or below the open third string. There are several things to think about at this point. How comfortable are you moving out of first position? How dark does the guitar sound if you get the melody down low in the bass, with the harmony notes even lower? Let's experiment with different keys to see what might work.

THE KEY OF A

In the key of A, the highest note of "If I Only Had a Brain" is a G♯, located at the fourth fret of the first string. That's not far away from the end-of-the-neck comfort zone—a nice start. The lowest note is an E at the second fret of the fourth string. The key of A stretches our normal melody range a bit on both the top and the bottom. Let's put some chords to it and see how it sounds and how playable it is.

Example 1 shows you the opening melodic phrase in the key of A. Most players will immediately run into a fingering problem in measure 2, where a Dmaj7 chord is required with a C♯ melody note on the second string. Another challenging part of this measure is reaching the G♯ note in the melody while trying to sustain the rest of the D chord. In measure 3, the melody has descended to the fourth string, with an A chord underneath it. For most intermediate players, the required fingering—with the ring and little fingers fretting the two bass strings—is too difficult.

After you've worked through these passages, play through the rest of Example 1 and see what you think. You'll quickly understand why I tried another key!

Successful arrangements not only sound good but are playable as well.

TRACK
65   Introduction

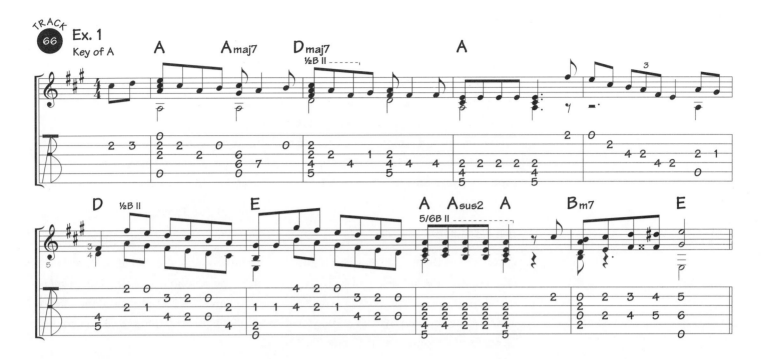

THE KEY OF G

In the key of G, the highest note of the melody, *ti,* is an F♯ at the second fret of the first string. The lowest note, *sol,* is the open fourth string. The melody stays in first position in this key, which is an advantage for many intermediate players. But will the sound get too bass-heavy when the melody goes all the way down to D? Are there other problems? Let's take a look.

Example 2 shows the first melodic phrase of the tune in G. The first problem is the third melody note, a D on the second string with a G chord under it. The fingering eliminates the third from the G chord (the note that makes it a major chord—a B at the open second string) unless you play it on the fifth string at the second fret, or the third string, fourth fret.

Fingerstyle guitarists must be careful about including the fifth-string B and the sixth-string G in a G chord. The two low frequencies can sound muddy together. Playing one of those two notes up an octave usually solves the problem. In this case, I wanted the root note G in the bass, because this is the first time the listener hears the chord, and root position is the strongest voicing. So the B must go up an octave—to the fourth fret, third string, in Example 2, creating a bright chord voicing.

The rest of the arrangement is workable, although it gets pretty low-pitched in measure 3. If you decide to use this key but think that the arrangement is too low-pitched, capo the guitar up a few frets to brighten up the sound. But let's keep experimenting.

THE KEY OF E

In the key of E you can play the entire melody in first position, but it is even lower-pitched than it is in the key of G. The range is from the second fret of the fifth string up to the fourth fret of the second string. Example 3 shows the first phrase of the melody in E. It's not particularly easy to play, with the little finger stretching to the fourth fret. The tone of the guitar is also quite dark.

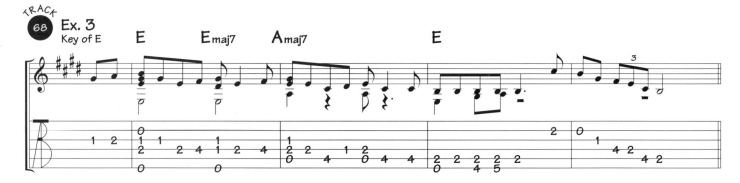

As an experiment, I moved the melody up a full octave (see Example 4). It's still in the key of E. This version has considerably more possibilities than Example 3. If I were working on an advanced arrangement, I would give the key of E thorough consideration. It has the advantage of having an open-string root note in the bass for two of the most important chords in the key: E and A. But before we get too far into E, let's try the last major guitar-friendly key: C.

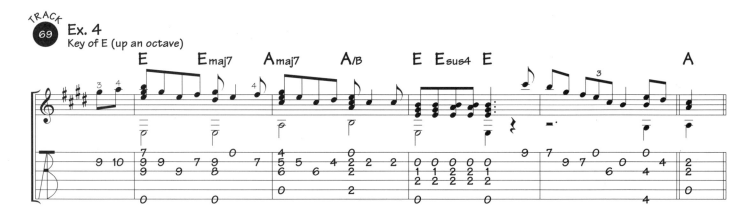

THE KEY OF C

The melodic range of "If I Only Had a Brain" in the key of C goes down to the normal low note of our range parameter: the open third string. The highest note is at the seventh fret of the first string. The chord fingerings in this key are easy to play, and the pitch of the melody is in a nice range. Also, when the melody goes up the neck a bit, it is easy to harmonize it with parallel sixths on the third string.

These realizations made me decide to pursue the key of C for this arrangement. Example 5 shows you the basic arrangement. Take some time to play through it so that when you get to Example 6 you will understand the changes I made to increase its technical level and its appeal.

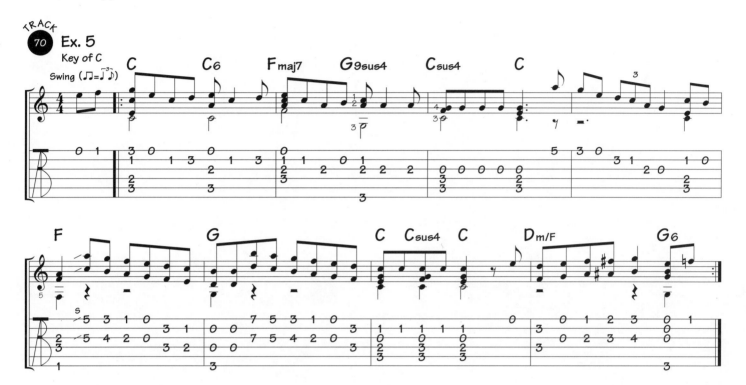

THE AABA SONG FORM

Fingerstyle arrangers must be aware of the song form they are dealing with. "If I Only Had a Brain" is in AABA form, often called "Tin Pan Alley song form." It is a 32-measure form broken into four sections. The first two sections consist of the same eight-measure melody, the third eight-bar section—often called the bridge—uses a new melody, and the final eight bars use the melody from the first section. Many of the great tunes of the big-band era were written in this form, including "Bye-Bye Blackbird," "I Got Rhythm," and "Satin Doll" (see page 60).

When you sing different lyrics from section to section in an AABA song, you can get away with repeating the same musical accompaniment. But in fingerstyle guitar solos there aren't any lyrics, so you need to vary the arrangement from one section to the next to keep it from becoming repetitious. Since you are not allowed to change the melody (can you write a better melody than Harold Arlen?), something else in the arrangement needs to change. In this tune, I chose to work with the bass line. I came up with three different bass lines for the three times through the A section. This keeps the listeners on their toes.

INSIDE THE ARRANGEMENT

In measures 1–4 of Example 6, I harmonized the melody with a slow-moving bass line, moving mostly in half notes. I included a chromatic bass movement and a half-dimin-

If I Only Had a Brain

Music by Harold Arlen, arranged by Mark Hanson

ished chord (Am/F#) to spice up the harmony a bit. For variety, I also added a high C note to the single-line fill in measures 3 and 4. Measures 5–6 contain an ascending bass line under the descending melody. This is a very strong harmonization technique, called contrary motion. The bass line consists of simple arpeggiated F and G chords. The fingering is surprisingly easy, and it sounds great. This section is repeated in measures 13–15. The arpeggiated chord idea continues in the bass during the second A section in measures 9–11, starting on a low E note under the C chord.

In the bridge (measures 17–24), the moving bass line acts as a fill during pauses in the melody. I didn't worry about a constantly moving bass line in this section because the new melody and harmony provided enough fresh ideas.

In the final eight bars (measures 25–32), the bass line is in descending quarter notes starting on an E note on the fourth string. This works as an alternative to the root note C because of the final chord in measure 24. The note on the fourth string of that G7 chord is an F (the seventh of the chord), which needs to resolve down to the E to maintain proper voice leading in the G7-to-C chord change. This particular descending bass line works great in the key of C. It descends a full octave and lands on the lowest note of the guitar: the open E sixth string.

The key of C works out beautifully for this tune. But remember, a good player can play a tune in any key on the guitar. For acoustic fingerstyle players who use a lot of open strings, some keys work much better than others. It is your job as arranger to ferret out the key that sounds the best and is the most playable.

Arranging Piano Music

Dale Miller

Many traditional fingerpicking guitar techniques are very pianistic. The most obvious example is the fingerpicker's steady alternating thumb, which is similar to (and was probably borrowed from) the ragtime or stride pianist's steady left hand. Huddie Ledbetter, who admitted to spending hours sitting next to barrelhouse piano players, used many boogie-woogie bass lines for his rockin' 12-string guitar style. Blind Blake's print advertisements often mention his "piano sounding guitar."

While Leadbelly, Blake, and other traditional pickers almost surely absorbed piano techniques in a folky, right-brain sort of way, by playing along with piano players or piano records and letting the piano licks and style creep into their playing organically, many of today's guitarists use a more academic, left-brain approach. They purchase piano sheet music, sit down with manuscript paper and pencil or music-writing software, and work out a guitar arrangement. In this lesson, we'll concentrate on the left-brain approach, but you should keep in mind that the more instinctive method sometimes works out better and that much of the knowledge you gain by going through the drudgery of working with sheet music can eventually become instinctive.

CHALLENGES IN TRANSCRIBING

There are some obvious limitations to the guitar's ability to play piano music. The first is that the guitar doesn't have a piano's range. Luckily the missing notes fall at the two extreme ends of the piano keyboard, though this isn't immediately obvious since guitar music is written in the treble clef only, an octave higher than it actually sounds.

This difference in range is seldom a major hindrance and is often not a factor at all; the biggest change you might have to make is moving a bass note up an octave.

A bigger problem is that as a guitarist you're limited in the number of notes you can play at once. Obviously, it's never possible to play more than six notes at the same time, but in practice you're often limited to only three or four notes because your lowest note is on the fourth or fifth string and you want an octave or more separation between it and the rest of the chord, and/or because your left-hand fingers just can't stretch and bend enough to get in all the notes of the original piano chord. Deciding which notes to include is one of the key skills of good transcription. In general, you need to include the "weirder" notes: the ninths, flatted fifths, suspended fourths, etc. You can feel confident about omitting the more "normal" notes, such as octaves, perfect fifths, and major thirds; the listener fills in these missing notes from memory and even hears them as part of the overtone series of the bass note.

Another skill you need to develop is deciding to which key to transcribe the piano arrangement. This is your first decision, and it's one you must be willing to change even after you've put some time into the project. This process can be greatly simplified by using a computer. Modern music-writing software allows you to transcribe (and transpose keys) instantly and generate tablature in standard or open tunings.

Keep in mind that each key has a "personality," especially in the first position on the guitar.

Introduction

CHOOSING A KEY

In choosing a key, you should first be aware that solo fingerstyle transcriptions are almost always in C, G, D, A, E, or occasionally F. In these keys, many notes fall on open strings, making the arrangements easier to play. You need to consider the range of the tune. You don't want any melody note to be higher than the 14th or 15th fret or lower than the open third string. Next, check out sections that have clusters of melody notes played up the neck. Make sure you can find a way to fit in the correct bass notes under these runs. A tuning that allows these bass notes to fall on open strings is ideal.

You should also keep in mind that each key has a natural "personality," especially in the first position on the guitar. C, for example, is a very closed key with a high-pitched lowest tonic note. It lends itself well to the I–vi–ii–V progression in songs like "These Foolish Things." Guitaristic bass lines like the one shown in Example 1 fall easily in C. They define the chord progression, create some complexity and interest, and often have to carry the song since this tuning forces you to leave out many of the simple harmony notes from the original piano sheet music. Another potential problem with C is that you don't have open-string bass notes for the I, IV, and V chords. To avoid too many full barre chords when the melody drifts up the neck, you can use false harmonics, where you touch the string lightly with your right-hand index finger at the 12th fret (or 12 frets above where it's fretted) while plucking it with your right-hand ring finger. This works best when the melody notes are an octave above open-string notes (G, B, and E). You can't add harmony notes easily, but the sweet, sustaining chime-like harmonic notes create a lot of interest on their own, especially if you add an interesting bass line. I used this trick in transcribing "These Foolish Things," shown here in Example 2.

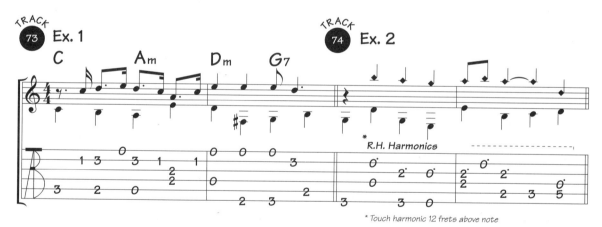

* Touch harmonic 12 frets above note

The key of D is a favorite of many guitarists. I remember one book of Scott Joplin transcriptions with every tune transcribed in that key. It's the only key in standard tuning or near-standard tuning with two open bass strings an octave apart in the open position. Either drop the low E string down to D or capo the first five strings at the second fret so that you're using D chord positions but playing in the concert key of E. The second approach means you can use standard barre-chord fingerings. Dropping the sixth string is better, though, if you need to play a bunch of notes above the fifth fret while fretting the low G note. The feel of D is totally different from C, in which the lowest tonic note is almost an octave higher. A tune that works well in D is "When the Red Red Robin Comes Bob Bob Bobbin' Along."

The key of E often works well for songs with full, lush chords. It's somewhat like D in that the lowest note on the instrument is the tonic, and it's quite different from C. I used this key for Gershwin's "Nice Work if You Can Get It."

The key of A is the one key in standard tuning where the I, IV, and V chords all have open strings in the bass. This offers some obvious advantages. I've used the key of A quite a bit for songs that have progressions with I–Idim7 changes, such as "You Took Advantage of Me" and "Ain't Misbehavin'."

My favorite key for transcribing is G. It has something of the feel of C with its opportunities for moving bass lines in the first position, but it also has an open string for the V chord (D). You can play some nice double-stops and even get up the neck a bit in the tonic G by bringing the left-hand thumb over the neck to finger the low G note at the third fret of the sixth string.

One of my favorite licks in this position is the one used by Blind Willie McTell in "Stomp Down Rider," shown in Example 3. I've adapted it for tunes like "Rockabye Your Baby to a Dixie Melody" and "Chattanooga Choo Choo." This thumb-over-the-top technique can also work well for runs in G involving the F♯, G, and A notes above middle C. That's what I did in the first two measures of "Whispering" (Example 4 below), which I transcribed in the key of G and played with a guitaristic alternating bass.

Sometimes an arrangement might be well served by an open tuning. When I arranged the lovely "Sweet Lorraine" more than 20 years ago, I finally chose open-E tuning. On slow tunes like this, it's very important to let the notes ring out. Hold the chords as long as possible and lift or move fingers only if you have to.

Supplement your hard work with some soulful loose playing to keep your sanity, but keep at it.

PLAYING AN ELLINGTON CLASSIC

The tune I've transcribed in full in this lesson is Duke Ellington's fabulous "Satin Doll." Ellington's fairly sparse sound works well for guitar, and you can see that surprisingly few notes are absent from the guitar arrangement. Notice the decisions I've made when I've had to leave something out and the few times I've thrown something in from left field. Don't be afraid to let the arrangement grow organically as you play it.

In this lesson, I've barely scratched the surface of this rich topic, but I hope I've given some inspiration. Arranging from sheet music can be frustrating, especially if your music-reading and writing skills are weak, but the rewards are great. Jump in. Supplement your hard work with some soulful loose playing to keep your sanity, but keep at it. Let your ear be your guide and don't be afraid to start over in a new key. Happy transcribing.

Satin Doll

Music and lyrics by Johnny Mercer, Duke Ellington, and Billy Strayhorn;
arranged by Dale Miller

Entertainment WEEKLY

OSCAR'S GRAND FINALE

No need to squelch your thoughts about Viggo Mortensen and his hobbit pals (or any other aspect of this year's Oscar ceremony). Talk about it with other EW readers in our pre- and postshow online discussion. Plus, get the complete winners list, picks for the 10 best and worst moments, and our backstage report at *ew.com/oscars.*

t
Y

E N

Fiddle to Fingerstyle

John Knowles

Not long ago, I set out to do a solo guitar arrangement of "Ashokan Farewell," Jay Ungar's haunting fiddle tune that became popular as the theme song of the PBS documentary *The Civil War*. When I translate a tune from one instrument to another, I do a lot of listening and a lot of experimenting. This time, I took notes on the process. I hope you can steal something from my general approach that will help you with your next project. The arrangement of the song appears at the end of this lesson.

I had heard "Ashokan Farewell" on the television series, but that kind of hearing is not good enough. When I am working on an arrangement, I want to know as much as possible about a tune before I actually sit down to work it out on the guitar. So I went to the Country Music Foundation's record collection, found it on a CD (*Songs of the Civil War*, Columbia 48607), and made a cassette dub. For about a week, I left the cassette in my car tape deck, and everywhere I went, I played it over and over.

Sometimes I just listened to it and thought about something else. Other times I listened in very specific ways. For instance, I remember singing the melody as each instrument played. I sang the bass line and listened for the chord changes. When I had that much figured out, I would sing variations on the melody or sing notes from the chords. I wanted to know my way around the world where the tune lived.

I wanted to know my way around the world where the tune lived.

LISTENING NOTES

During that time, I made several observations. Some of them may seem rather obvious, like the fact that the performance begins with solo fiddle (Jay Ungar) playing the tune all the way through. In a more subtle vein, I noticed that the fiddler changes the timing of the melody when the rhythm section comes in for the second pass through the tune. Some of those timing changes come naturally from the steady tempo provided by the rest of the band. But there are also rhythmic changes in some of the phrases.

I also noticed that when the guitarist (Russ Barenberg) plays the melody, he changes a couple of notes and plays different embellishments (slides, trills, etc.). He also changes octaves in the middle of the melody. The guitarist and the bassist (Molly Mason) usually play the same bass note, but not always. Finally, there is a great moment in the fiddle trio section (played by Ungar, Evan Stover, and Matt Glaser) where the rhythm stops and the trio holds a chord. All of these observations could affect my final arrangement.

At this point, I had a pretty good idea of the melody, the bass line, and the chords, but I had no idea what key the musicians were playing in. Since I don't have perfect pitch, I just imagined they were playing in C and tried to figure out where things would be. I knew I could always transpose to another key later.

Introduction

VISUALIZING FINGERINGS

I tried to visualize where my fingers would be to get the sounds I heard coming from the cassette. I know I shouldn't do this on the freeway, but there I was with my second finger on the eighth fret of the second string. That G is the first of two eighth-note pickups into the first bar of the melody.

Before long, I could tell that I would never be able to reach all of the melody notes and still play the bass line—not to mention the chords. That was when I realized that the melody covered about two octaves. I guess that's no big deal on a fiddle, but on a guitar it means a lot of shifting and not much room for chords. After all, the guitar has only three octaves plus whatever you can reach beyond the 12th fret.

I put out so much effort imagining that the recording was in the key of C that I started to believe it. Later when I sat down to play along with the cassette, I was momentarily stunned—the recording was in D.

LEARNING THE CHORDS

I know I shouldn't do this on the freeway, but there I was with my second finger on the eighth fret of the second string.

I played along with the recording in D until I could play the chords all the way through. I tried to play the same chord inversions that I heard. When I had to choose, I usually went with Mason's bass note, since it was typically lower and seemed to affect the sound more. That meant I was not always duplicating Barenberg's part.

I especially remember the feeling of playing chords behind the opening solo fiddle. The tempo is not perfectly even, but the imperfections taught me a lot about the phrasing of the melody. I knew I would be playing my arrangement as a solo, so I could afford the luxury of stretching the time where it felt like it needed it.

Well, that was great fun, but the assignment was to work out a fingerstyle solo version of "Ashokan Farewell." I had to leave the comfort of playing along with the recording in D and venture into unknown territory.

I poked around in several keys before I settled on A. I thought about tuning the sixth string down to D and playing in G or D. I made a pass at E and even C just to be sure. At this stage, I would have liked to have had several choices so that I could have made my decision based on which key sounded the best or felt the best on the fingerboard.

FILLING IN AROUND THE MELODY

In the end, I was pretty much forced into the key of A by the two-octave melody range and my desire to leave the bass line in good shape. So I sketched out an arrangement in A with just the melody and a bass line. At this point, I was not listening to the recording anymore. It's not that I had memorized everything; I wanted to leave some room for creative solutions that might be blocked if I were busy trying to get every detail just right. After all, I could always fix it later.

Next, I started to fill in a few chord notes between the melody and the bass line. I had to be careful here. I didn't want to grab a great chord at the expense of the phrasing. If you take a look at the music at the end of this lesson, you will see how I dealt with the problem. I have written the arrangement out like classic guitar notation, with the stems on the melody notes pointing up and the stems on the accompaniment pointing down.

In the first three bars, the melody does not move on the second beat. I decided to put chords on the second beat, so that the accompaniment moved from bass to chord to nothing on the three beats. If you examine the rest of the arrangement, you'll see that I have mostly followed this idea of letting the accompaniment move when the melody doesn't. In a sense, the tempo and the feeling of 1-2-3 are being conveyed by the combination of melody and accompaniment.

Of course, this also means that the harmony is being conveyed by that same combination. For example, in the first two beats of measure 14, the melody is an E and a C♯, while the accompaniment has an A and an E. Between the two, you hear an A chord (A, C♯, and E).

After several days of playing through my arrangement, I decided it was time to go back and consult the recording. Oops! I had left out one of the best bass notes. I had to find a way to get the F♯ on the downbeat of measure 6. I would've loved to have gone for the F♯ on the second fret of the sixth string, but it was a little far from that melody note on the ninth fret of the first string.

If you check out the tab for measures 5 and 6, you will see that I played three notes in a row on the third string to get from the F♯ on the ninth fret of the fifth string. I had to practice that shift to get it smooth, but now that I've got it, I really like it.

I referred earlier to the possibility of creative solutions. I took a little liberty with the melody in measure 17. The fiddle can sustain a long note and sound delicious, but a long note on an acoustic guitar just dies out. Those three eighth notes fill in for the missing sustain.

At times, I will play through the arrangement with a free tempo, as if someone were humming the tune while going about their chores. Other times, I will play it with a more even tempo, as if a young couple were dancing to the music.

ADDING FINAL TOUCHES

When I had almost completed my arrangement, I had a chance to talk with Jay Ungar about it. I incorporated several of his ideas about the bass line and harmony into my final version. He pointed out that there are other ways to harmonize the phrase that begins in measure 15, but the movement from A to F♯m to E gives the tune a distinct flavor. I think it's one of the reasons that "Ashokan Farewell" sounds old enough to be a real Civil War tune.

There are several issues that I have not resolved for myself yet. Although I have not written it out here, I have considered beginning the arrangement with a single-string version of the melody. I could play the whole thing or just the first 16 bars. Of course, I would embellish it like Ungar and Barenberg did.

I know that I will continue to experiment with different fingerings and an occasional new harmony note. Maybe I will find a way to work in that cool chord that the fiddle trio plays. It would replace the G chord in measure 20. I could add an A on the second fret of the third string to get G add 9. Hmmm . . .

I go through a process more or less like the one I have described here every time I work out a new arrangement. Each tune presents its own problems . . . make that opportunities. Along the way, I have found that composing for the guitar feels a lot like arranging the music you hear in your head. In any event, the more you do it, the better you get. And you can't hurt yourself trying!

Ashokan Farewell

Music by Jay Ungar, arranged by John Knowles

Easy Alternate Tunings

Dylan Schorer

Altered tunings can be beautiful and terrifying things. What they giveth in rich new voicings and sonorities, they taketh away in comprehension of the fingerboard. All the scale, arpeggio, and chord fingerings that you memorized through hours of practice and study are rendered useless in the new tuning—you are back to hunting and pecking for harmonies and melodies like a novice, or arduously building shapes using theoretical analysis.

Some players like altered tunings for exactly this reason—to disconnect themselves from what they know—but others don't want to leave the familiar ground of standard tuning totally behind. For these latter players, there is a family of tunings that offer a middle ground. These tunings change only one or two bottom strings, a small variation from standard tuning that still gives some deep new sounds to work with and also releases soloists from the ball and chain of playing only the melody notes within easy reach of a fretted bass note. These tunings have other significant advantages for performers: they're easy to get into and out of during a set, and they don't cause nearly as many retuning problems and broken strings as do alternate tunings that change the top (especially the third) strings.

The most popular of these tunings is dropped-D, with only the bottom string lowered one whole step to D. This tuning offers new sonic territory, but all you know about chords and scales still works for you on the five unaltered strings. And you only need to remember to move the notes you know on the bottom string up two frets.

Inspiring new sounds not far from the comfort of standard tuning.

G6 TUNING

Introduction   **TRACK 80**

Another popular tuning drops the fifth string down to G and the sixth down to D. The resulting tuning of D G D G B E, often called G6 tuning, is used frequently by performers like Chet Atkins ("Both Sides Now") and Adrian Legg ("Nanci"). To get there from standard tuning, simply drop your sixth string until it sounds in unison (one octave lower) with the fourth string (D). Then lower the fifth string until it matches the third string (G). It's not much of a revelation that this tuning works well for the key of G. You can have a low-G bass note sustaining or alternating with the D strings while you play melodies anywhere on the neck (see Example 1).

TRACK 81   Tuning: D G D G B E
Ex. 1

Now let's build some of the chords we need. For a G chord, use the notes of a regular open G chord on the top four strings but get the bass note with the open fifth string, as shown in the chord below. You can also play a piece of any G chord anywhere up the neck over the low-G bass note, as shown in the next three chords.

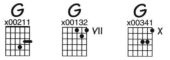

With these tools, you should be able to locate any chord you'll need.

The D doesn't need to change at all, because it is already confined to the top four strings. However, you can add the low-D bass. When fingerpicking you can play it like this D chord—just don't play the fifth string.

If you're strumming, you'll need to fret the fifth string at the second fret (A), as shown in the D chords below.

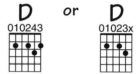

You'll probably need a C chord as well. Look at your open C chord in standard tuning. You'll need to raise the bass note on the fifth string up two frets, but that would make quite a stretch. While fingerpicking you could omit the C note on the second string and use this shape.

A better option may be to use a barre at the fifth fret—it's like a standard-tuning C barre chord with the bass note raised two frets. Also, mute or don't play the first string, or fret the high C at the eighth fret, as shown in the examples below. Note that this chord is movable; at the sixth fret it becomes a C♯ chord, at the seventh a D, etc.

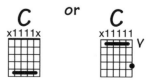

Take a look at the following chords and consider how each relates to its standard tuning counterpart.

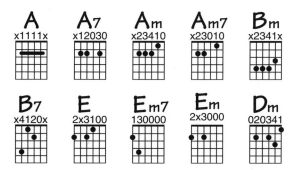

Below are a couple more movable barre chords that will allow you to obtain any other major or minor chord you need:

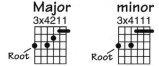

So far, we've been searching for ways to play familiar chords, but the exciting things about these tunings are the entirely new sounds available. Example 2 shows some nice voicings in various contexts. With these tools, you should be able to locate any chord you'll need. Try transferring a familiar song that you play in the key of G to this tuning.

DOWN TO C

This exciting tuning is similar to the last, but the sixth string drops to C (C G D G B E). After you've lowered the fifth string to G, drop the sixth string until its seventh-fret harmonic matches the 12th-fret harmonic on the fifth string to fine-tune it. This is a very useful tuning that has been used by many players. Lindsey Buckingham plays the Fleetwood Mac song "Never Going Back Again" in this tuning. Some other examples of this tuning include Richard Thompson's "1952 Vincent Black Lightning," Chet Atkins' "Just as I Am," and Duck Baker's arrangement of "Swing Low, Sweet Chariot."

Some of the greatest sounds in this tuning are the truly huge C chords available.

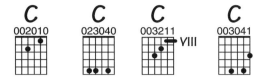

These voicings sound great as the tonic in the key of C, or especially cool as a big IV chord when playing in G. Obviously, all of the voicings we learned for the last tuning that were confined to the top five strings will work in this tuning as well. Here are a few new chords that are specific to this tuning:

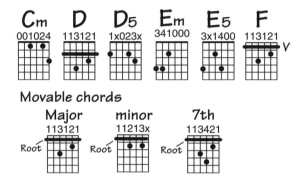

Example 3 shows a few progressions and grooves available in this tuning. The song "Raindance" that follows this lesson ties together many of these ideas.

MAKING UP YOUR OWN TUNINGS

When creating solo arrangements of melodies that remain on the top strings, it's helpful to tune the bottom strings to the most commonly needed bass notes for a particular tune. For instance, the tuning F G D G B E works well for the large group of Celtic tunes in the G mixolydian mode (G major scale with an F♮ instead of an F♯). Beppe Gambetta plays his signature piece "Slow Creek" in this tuning. Example 4 puts this tuning to use. When you play it, you'll need to use judicious right- or left-hand damping to prevent the G and F bass strings from ringing together.

Tuning: F G D G B E

Ex. 4

There are many other tunings to experiment with—dropping only the sixth string to C can create some satisfying sounds, as can raising the fifth string to B♭. Or do the limbo with your sixth string and see how low it can go—down to A or B can be pretty powerful. The possibilities are endless.

Raindance

Music by Dylan Schorer

Open-D Tuning

Mark Hanson

Many of the most common guitar tunings used today are relatively recent inventions. Contemporary players like John Fahey, Davey Graham (who invented D A D G A D), the late Michael Hedges, and even the pop group Sonic Youth have added volumes to the alternate tunings library. But one of the richest-sounding and easiest-to-use tunings has been a mainstay in the tunings archives for more than a century: open-D tuning.

A composition entitled "Sebastopol" by Henry Worrall was published in the late 19th century, using open-D tuning (made up of the notes of a D-major chord: D A D F♯ A D, lowest pitch to highest). That piece, along with an open-G tuning piece entitled "Spanish Fandango," became a staple of the parlor guitar repertoire of the period.

In the early 1900s, open-D tuning (known as "Sebastopol" or "Vestapol" tuning) became one of the most commonly used tunings for guitarists playing slide guitar. The convenience of producing a major chord without fretting any strings, and producing other major chords by simply laying a slide straight across all of the strings, made it exceedingly attractive to players. The tuning and its title became so pervasive among blues guitarists that blues archivist Stefan Grossman named his Vestapol video company after it.

Today, open-D tuning and its many variants (among them: open D minor, D A D F A D; open D major7, D A D F♯ A C♯; and open D7, D A D F♯ A C) are used in many styles of music. You will find them used by blues and slide players (Ry Cooder, John Lee Hooker), folksingers (Joni Mitchell, Richie Havens), contemporary fingerstylists (Leo Kottke, Alex de Grassi, William Ackerman, John Fahey, Martin Simpson), and even rock bands (Allman Brothers, Eagles).

The sidebar in this lesson, "Songs in Open D," lists a wide variety of these tunes.

One of the richest and easiest-to-use tunings has been a mainstay in the tunings archives for more than a century.

Introduction and Tune-up

GETTING IN TUNE

To produce open-D tuning from standard tuning, start by tuning the first and sixth strings down one whole step from E to D. Next, tune the second string down one whole step from B to A. Finally, tune the third string down one half step from G to F♯.

To check your tuning, simply strum the open strings. Does it sound like a major chord? If not, tune it again, this time matching unisons: the seventh fret of the bass string equals the open fifth string; the fifth fret of the fifth string equals the open fourth; the fourth fret of the fourth string equals the open third; the third fret of the third string equals the open second; and the fifth fret of the second string equals the open first.

Try committing these fret positions to memory. It is easy to remember which frets you use on several strings; they simply match the number of the string: third fret/third string, fourth fret/fourth string, fifth fret/fifth string. The bass string uses the seventh fret, which is the same as drop-D tuning. The first and second strings are the same distance (a perfect fourth) from each other as they are in standard tuning. So you use the fifth fret of the second string to match the open first, just as you do in standard tuning.

Getting chord tunings like open D exactly in tune can be frustrating. The frustration lies in fine-tuning the strings well enough so that the chords actually sound in tune.

Assuming that you have a quality guitar with relatively new strings, the trick to getting alternate tunings in tune is to make sure that the octaves and unisons match perfectly.

Here is one method of fine-tuning open-D tuning: Fret the fifth and second strings at the fifth fret. Working in pairs, pick all of the strings except the third (the F#). All five of these notes are D, in three different octaves. They should all ring nicely together. Once those are in tune, fret the third string at the eighth fret. Does that pitch equal the open first string? It should.

At first you are likely to have some trouble fine-tuning the guitar in an open tuning. Don't despair. I have seen some of the biggest names in the acoustic guitar world struggle to tune their guitars on stage or play with the guitar less than perfectly in tune. It happens to everyone.

Open-E tuning (E B E G# B E, low to high), another variant of open D, has the same relationships from string to string as open D but is tuned one whole step higher. This puts additional stress on the guitar (three strings are tuned higher than standard) and produces a brighter sound. But such a tuning might not be advisable for your particular instrument. If you need to play in open E, consider tuning to open D and placing a capo at the second fret.

SCALES IN OPEN D

Because of its relatively limited fretting requirements, open D major can be among the simplest tunings to use on the guitar.

The advantages of playing in open-D tuning are many. You can play the usual tonic chord, D major, by simply strumming the open strings. Other useful chords can be played by simply adding one or two fingers or by fretting a simple barre. You can fret melodies on a single string while playing harmony notes on the open strings.

The drawbacks, as in all altered tunings, are that the chord and scale positions are different from what you might be accustomed to in standard tuning. Plus, in an open tuning it may not always be as easy to play in keys other than the key of the tuning—D major in the case of open-D tuning.

Most tunes in open-D tuning are played in the key of D. With this in mind, let's take a look at some scale positions for D major. Example 1 diagrams a D-major scale at the end of the neck, using all of the open strings. Examples 2 and 3 diagram a D-major scale in higher positions on the neck. Because the bass strings are tuned a fifth apart, the fingerings in Examples 2 and 3 require serious stretching or the use of an open string.

Ex. 1

Ex. 2

Ex. 3

The keys of G and A are also quite workable in open-D tuning. Example 4 diagrams a G-major scale at the end of the neck. Example 5 diagrams an A-major scale at the end of the neck. If you are a recreational player, I would suggest that you not spend too much time working on the scales located up the neck. For you, the beauty of this tuning is likely to be in the chords you can produce, rather than the scales.

One of the main attractions of playing in most open tunings is the beautiful chords you can produce without much effort on the part of your fretting hand.

Ex. 4

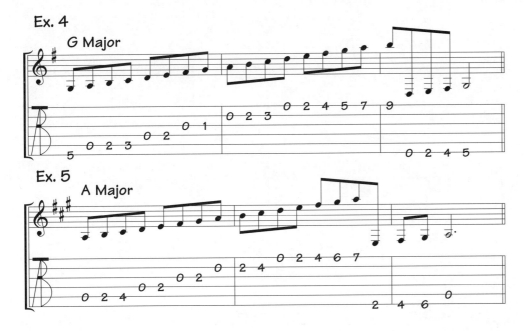

Ex. 5

CHORD FORMS

One of the main attractions of playing in most open tunings is the beautiful chords you can produce without too much effort on the part of your fretting hand. Playing simple major and minor chords is easy in most open-chord tunings, but adding some other notes to your basic chords can make open tunings sound especially rich.

A quick music theory lesson is in order here, so that you understand chord structure a bit. A major or minor chord consists of three notes: the first, third, and fifth notes of a major or minor scale (*do re mi fa sol la ti*). If you play those three notes together, voilà!

You have a chord. (A six-string major or minor chord on the guitar really has only three notes, which are doubled or tripled at different octaves.) You can make these three-note chords sound much richer by adding other notes of the scale (*re, fa, la,* and *ti*) to those three. This is where open tunings really shine.

In open-D tuning, the open strings already provide the *do, mi,* and *sol* of a D-major chord. To add other notes (sixths, sevenths, ninths, and 11ths) to this D chord, all you need to do is fret a note or two (or five!) somewhere on the neck.

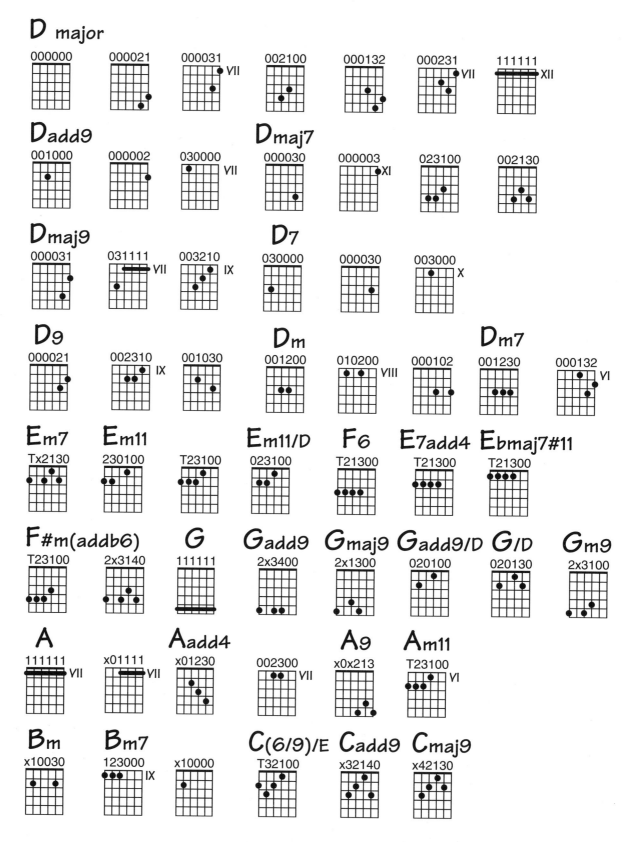

On the previous page, I have diagrammed numerous chord fingerings that work beautifully in this tuning. I have organized them by their letter names, so that you have a choice of voicings for each chord.

Make up some chord progressions—such as Em–A–D, or Em–F♯m–G–A–Bm—and experiment with the different voicings I have provided for each chord as you move from one to the next. Which voicings move smoothly from one to another? Which don't? Paying attention to what sounds good in your experiments will be a valuable lesson in voice leading.

Some of the chords in the diagram are not in the key of D major: Dm, D7, D9, C, F, E, and E♭. However, these chords are commonly used in key-of-D pieces. Try playing the F–E–E♭ chords consecutively, followed by an open D chord. There is some serious dissonance here, especially in the E and E♭ chords. But the listener's ear won't mind because the drone strings provide a constancy.

As you develop your composing skills, you will learn that you can get away with vertical dissonance (a chord that is dissonant) if the horizontal lines (the melody, for instance) are smooth and make sense. You will also learn that an amazing amount of harmonic change and dissonance is acceptable when the chords are connected by a common tone, a note that occurs in adjacent chords. Give it a try. If you don't like the sound of some of the dissonances at first, I suspect they will grow on you as you experiment with them.

An amazing amount of harmonic change and dissonance is acceptable when the chords are connected by a common tone.

SLIDE IN OPEN D

To play slide guitar in open D, you will find that the most commonly played chords are open D, plus full barres at the fifth fret (a G chord), seventh fret (an A), and 12th fret (high-octave D). These positions correspond to the I, IV, and V chords of the key. To make a slide tune sound bluesy, often the chords at the third fret and tenth fret are incorporated into the tune. These chords correspond to the lowered third and seventh notes of a D scale.

Also, when playing slide, try placing your slide one fret below each of these positions and sliding up to the normal position (for instance: slide second fret to third; sixth fret to seventh; 11th to 12th; etc.). It doesn't take a lot of effort to make open-D tuning sound bluesy with a slide.

"AMAZING GRACE"

The arrangement of "Amazing Grace" in this lesson is a simple one, yet it uses some of the attributes of open-D tuning to good effect. The arrangement is built largely on an ascending arpeggio picked by the thumb. Consider fretting the D7 chord in measure 2 with three separate fingers—the pinky, ring, and middle—so that the index finger is free to fret the subsequent melody note on the second fret of the first string. With this fingering, you will be able to sustain the second- and third-string notes as the melody changes on the first string.

The G chord in measure 3 is fingered exactly like a first-position E7 chord in standard tuning. Add the second-string melody note with your ring finger.

Like the D7 chord in measure 2, the Dmaj7 chord in measure 6 should be fingered with the pinky, ring, and middle fingers. This again allows the index finger to fret the second-fret melody note on the first string as you sustain the second- and third-string notes. The barre chord in measure 7 is an Asus4. Finger the third string with the middle finger.

In measure 8, you should finger the ninth-fret note with the ring finger. Try to sustain this note as you release the barre and prepare to fret the first note of measure 9. Sustaining the final melody note in measure 8 until the first beat of measure 9 will help make the melody flow.

Measure 12 has a lovely descending middle voice. To make this passage as effective as it can be, mute the sixth string on the first beat of measure 13. That gives you a root-position Bm chord, rather than a Bm with a low D still ringing from the previous measure. I mute the sixth string by lightly touching it with my left thumb or by touching it with the base of the thumb of my picking hand.

To embellish this piece, try arpeggiating it with eighth notes instead of quarter notes. Also, make sure that you have your guitar nicely in tune before you play this or any piece in open-D tuning.

"Amazing Grace" is lots of fun to play, and it's quite easy. Once you get it, play around with some of the other chord fingerings shown in the diagram. With a little bit of practice, you may even learn how to improvise a bit in open-D tuning. Have fun!

SONGS IN OPEN D

William Ackerman, "Ely," *In Search of the Turtle's Navel*, Windham Hill 1001.

Allman Brothers, "Little Martha," *Eat a Peach*, Polydor 823654. Open E.

Duck Baker, "A Pretty Fair Miss," *American Traditional*, Day Job 1. Day Job, 570 25th St., Richmond, CA 94804.

Ry Cooder, "Thirteen Question Method," *Get Rhythm*, Warner 25639.

Ry Cooder, "Vigilante Man," *Ry Cooder*, Warner 6402. Open E.

Alex de Grassi, "Alpine Medley," *Turning: Turning Back*, Windham Hill 1004. Open E.

John Fahey, "Poor Boy a Long Way from Home," *Return of the Repressed*, Rhino 71737.

Ed Gerhard, "Howl," *Luna*, Virtue 1921. Virtue Records, PO Box 532, Newmarket, NH 03857.

Mark Hanson, "Silent Night," *Yuletide Guitar*, Accent on Music 6044. Accent on Music, 19363 Willamette Dr. #252, West Linn, OR 97068.

David Hidalgo, "Little King of Everything," *Ferrington Guitars CD*, HarperCollins Publishers and Callaway Editions.

John Lee Hooker, "Terraplane Blues," *The Ultimate Collection*, Rhino 70572.

Leo Kottke, "Little Martha," *A Shout Toward Noon*, Private/Windham Hill 2007. Lowered one half step to open Db.

Leo Kottke, "Watermelon," *6- and 12-String Guitar*, Rhino 71612. Lowered one step to open C.

Peter Lang, "When Kings Come Home," *Leo Kottke/John Fahey/Peter Lang*, Takoma Fantasy TAK-6502. Fantasy, 10th and Parker, Berkeley, CA 94710.

Adrian Legg, "The Irish Girl," *Guitars and Other Cathedrals*, Relativity 1045.

Joni Mitchell, "Both Sides Now," *Clouds*, Reprise 6341.

Joni Mitchell, "Chelsea Morning," *Clouds*, Reprise 6341.

Harvey Reid, "Otto Wood," *Steel Drivin' Man*, Woodpecker 107. Woodpecker, PO Box 815, York, ME 03909.

Roy Rogers, "Tip-Walk," *Slidewinder*, Blind Pig 2687. Blind Pig, PO Box 2344, San Francisco, CA 94126.

Martin Simpson, "No Depression in Heaven," *The Collection*, Shanachie 79089. Shanachie, 13 Laight St., Sixth Floor, New York, NY 10013.

David Wilcox, "Wildberry Pie," *Home Again*, A&M 5357.

Amazing Grace

Music by John Newton, arranged by Mark Hanson

Tuning: D A D F# A D

Exploring D A D G A D

Mark Hanson

The beauty of alternate tunings is the opportunity they provide to create new chords and new voicings.

Introduction and Tune-up

Well over 30 years ago, English fingerstyle patriarch Davey Graham developed one of the most attractive and versatile alternate tunings for guitar: D A D G A D (commonly pronounced "dad gad"). Graham invented it while living in Morocco to facilitate his playing with oud players. Upon his return to England, the tuning quickly gained popularity among British guitarists playing traditional music, among them John Renbourn, Bert Jansch, and Jimmy Page. Later, D A D G A D became the tuning of choice for great French fingerstyle guitarist Pierre Bensusan.

One of D A D G A D's main attractions for guitarists is the rich, harplike sonorities that can be produced with relatively easy chord fingerings. Since it does not explicitly state a modality (as D major and G major tunings do, for instance), D A D G A D can be used to play in a variety of keys and modes.

The open strings of D A D G A D produce a D suspended-fourth chord (root, fourth, fifth). The third of a D scale (F♯ or F), which would peg the tuning as major or minor, is missing from the open strings. Because of that, guitarists can use D A D G A D as easily in the key of D minor as in D major. It is an effective tuning in the key of G, and it also works well for modal tunes and pieces with independent treble and bass lines.

To get into D A D G A D from standard tuning, lower your sixth string one whole step, from E to D. Also lower your second string a whole step, from B to A, and your first string a whole step, from E to D. To make sure your guitar is in tune in D A D G A D, match the seventh fret of the sixth string to the open fifth string, match the second fret of the third string to the open second string, and match the fifth fret of the second string (already tuned down) to the open first string.

SCALES AND CHORDS

An initial disadvantage of any alternate tuning for standard-tuning players is that the chord and scale fingerings are different from standard. Some alternate tunings, such as dropped-D (D A D G B E), are only slightly altered from standard tuning and don't take much effort to learn. Others are a bit further away from standard and consequently might take more work.

If you have trouble fathoming alternate tunings, it may help you to think of the four bass strings of D A D G A D as the same as dropped-D tuning. Or, if you prefer to compare D A D G A D to standard tuning, the chords and scales on the third, fourth, and fifth strings are the same.

In D A D G A D, the two treble strings have the same relationship to each other as they do in standard tuning and dropped-D: a perfect fourth (five frets) apart in pitch. They are simply tuned one whole step lower than standard. Any fingerings that you use in standard tuning will have to move two frets higher on the two treble strings in D A D G A D to produce the same sound.

If you approach D A D G A D in this manner, at least you will have a familiar basis from which to work. But don't get too hung up on trying to produce standard-tuning sounds with an alternate tuning. There will likely be times when you will want your voicings to sound the same as standard tuning; but the beauty of alternate tunings is the opportunity they provide to create new chords and new voicings, and to play scales with harp-like sustain. By being open to new chords and voicings, you will be able to take fuller advantage of an alternate tuning.

First we'll learn first-position scales for D major and D minor in D A D G A D tuning. Practice these scales until the positions are firmly in your brain and fingers. You will notice that both of these scales use all of the open strings. This will prove to be very convenient as you start building chords from these notes.

I have also diagrammed a variety of chords in D A D G A D for the keys of D major and D minor (see Example 1). In the key of D major, the main chords are D, Em, F♯m, G, A, and Bm. In the key of D minor, the main chords are Dm, F, Gm, Am, B♭, and C. For each chord, I have shown the fingering for a triad (root, third, fifth), plus harmonically rich variations that are easy to finger in this tuning. Perhaps some of these fingerings will inspire you to compose a tune or two!

There are limitless variations on these fingerings, of course. I have diagrammed just a few to get you started. After you master these, experiment with fingerings of your own. With a little effort, you will find some very rich chords that are easy to play.

Tuning: D A D G A D

Ex. 1

D Major

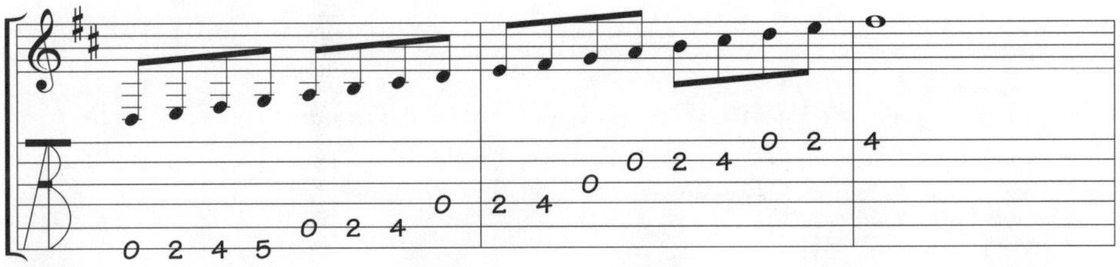
0 2 4 5 0 2 4 0 2 4 0 0 2 4 0 2 4

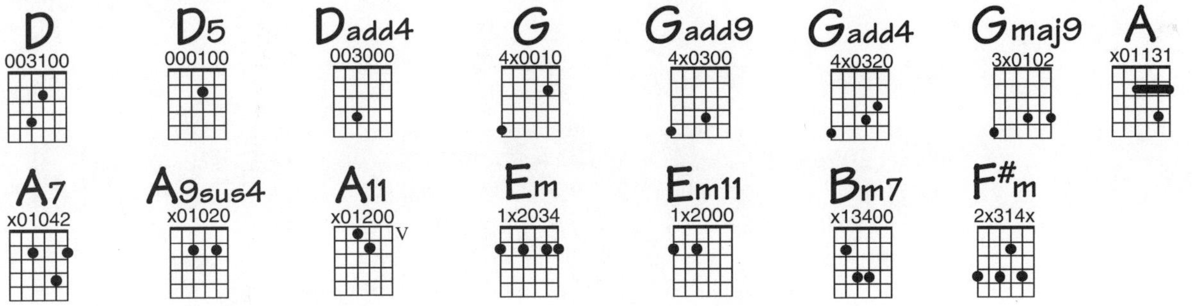
D
003100
D5
000100
Dadd4
003000
G
4x0010
Gadd9
4x0300
Gadd4
4x0320
Gmaj9
3x0102
A
x01131
A7
x01042
A9sus4
x01020
A11
x01200
V
Em
1x2034
Em11
1x2000
Bm7
x13400
F#m
2x314x

D Minor

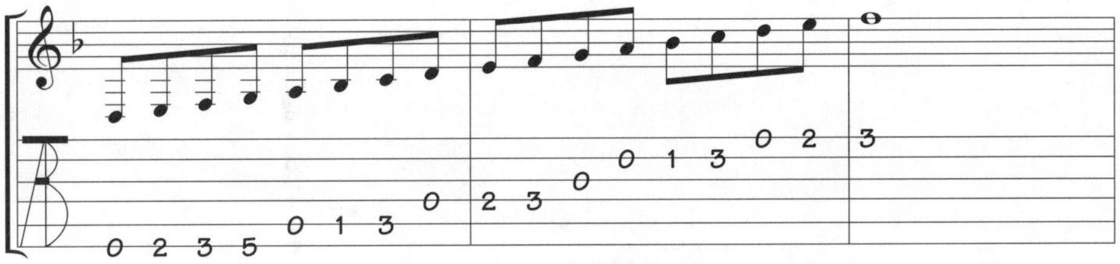
0 2 3 5 0 1 3 0 2 3 0 0 1 3 0 2 3

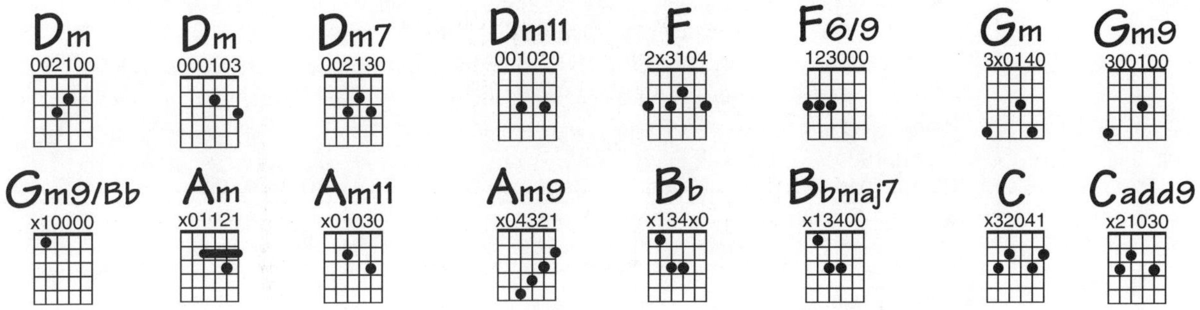
Dm
002100
Dm
000103
Dm7
002130
Dm11
001020
F
2x3104
F6/9
123000
Gm
3x0140
Gm9
300100
Gm9/Bb
x10000
Am
x01121
Am11
x01030
Am9
x04321
Bb
x134x0
Bbmaj7
x13400
C
x32041
Cadd9
x21030

After you have spent some time with D major and D minor, get accustomed to the key of G. First work on the G major scale below. The G major scale also uses all of the open strings in this tuning.

Next, work on key-of-G chord positions. The main chords are G, Am, Bm, C, D, and Em. Below you'll find several G, C, and D fingerings that work well in D A D G A D. You have already seen several other fingerings for G, C, and D in the chord diagrams for D major and D minor. Alternate fingerings for the other chords of the key of G (Am, Bm, and Em) can also be found in the D major and D minor diagrams.

In a minor key, the sixth and/or seventh notes of the scale are often played a half step higher than normal. This takes you into the realm of dorian mode and melodic and harmonic minor. Example 2 shows the D dorian scale (a D minor scale with the B♭ note raised to a B♮) to prepare you for my fingerstyle arrangement of "Twin Sisters." I have also included diagrams of the chords you will need for that tune.

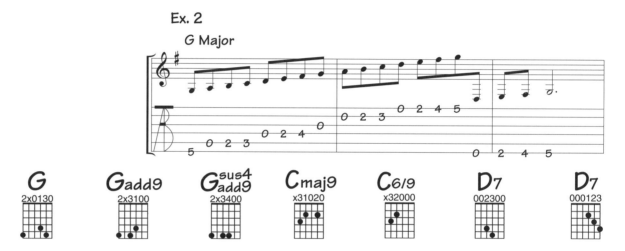

VARIATIONS ON D A D G A D

Englishman Martin Carthy produced a lower-tuned version of D A D G A D to better match the range of his singing voice. It is E A D E A E (lowest pitch to highest), commonly called "A-pipe" tuning. The relationships of the five lowest-pitched strings of Carthy's tuning are the same as the five highest-pitched strings of D A D G A D. All the fingerings are identical but moved one string lower. Once you have learned your chords and scales for D A D G A D, it is a relatively easy matter to play in A-pipe tuning as well.

Another interesting variation on D A D G A D can be produced using the Third Hand capo (made by the Third Hand Capo Company, PO Box 4662, Portsmouth, NH 03802). This elastic band–style capo allows you to create the D A D G A D sound from the open strings without retuning any strings. The Third Hand has six individual cams, which allow you to capo individual strings or groups of strings, while leaving other strings to vibrate from the nut.

To produce a D A D G A D sound with a Third Hand, capo the third, fourth, and fifth strings (G, D, and A) at the second fret. Leave the first, second, and sixth strings open to the nut. This actually produces E B E A B E, which is the equivalent of D A D G A D capoed at the second fret.

The advantage of using the Third Hand capo is that your scale fingerings and chord forms do not change from standard tuning, but you still have the advantages of the altered-tuning sound from the open strings. Essentially, you are still playing in standard tuning, but with the advantages of D A D G A D—like open strings. Fingerstylists Chris Proctor and Harvey Reid, among others, use the Third Hand capo to great effect.

D Dorian

"Twin Sisters" Chord Diagrams

"TWIN SISTERS"

At the end of this lesson, you'll find the first 20 measures of "Twin Sisters," a tune that Doc and Merle Watson recorded on *Down South* (Sugar Hill 3742). Doc flatpicked the tune, while Merle played clawhammer banjo. Merle used "mountain minor" tuning, the banjo's equivalent of D A D G A D. (The full arrangement of "Twin Sisters" can be found in Mark Hanson's book *The Art of Solo Fingerpicking,* Accent on Music.)

Twin Sisters

Traditional, arranged by Mark Hanson

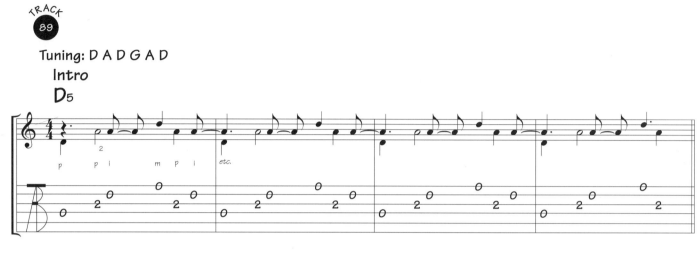

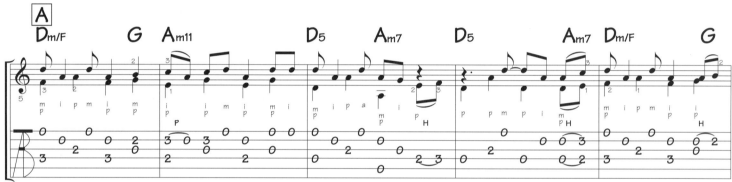

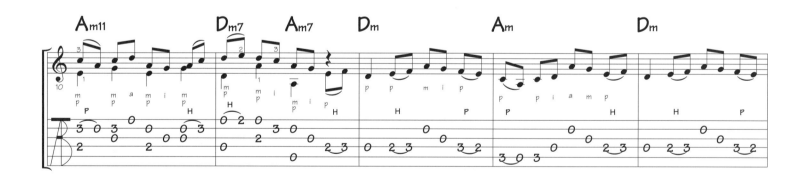

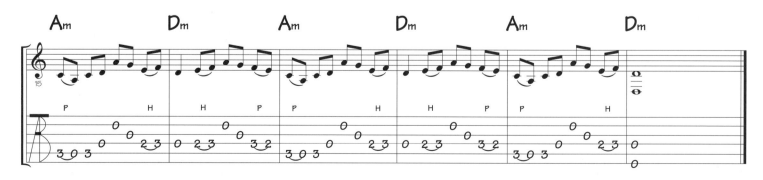

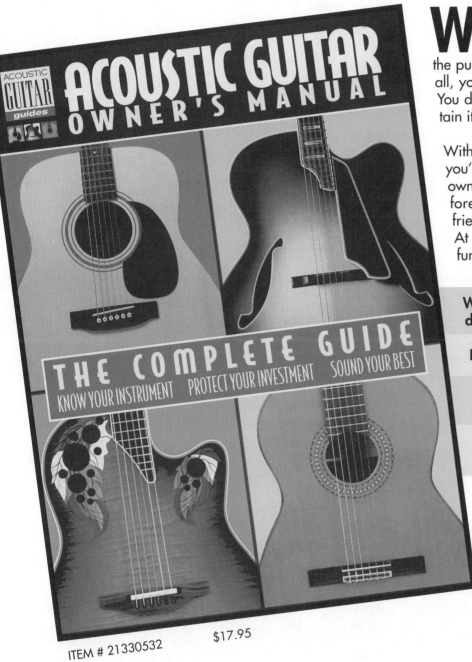

Other Titles from String Letter Publishing

Also Available in the Acoustic Guitar CD Songbook Series

Each title has a CD with original artist recordings plus a book with complete guitar transcriptions. All include songs in both standard and alternate tunings.

FINGERSTYLE GUITAR MASTERPIECES

John Williams • Adrian Legg • Chris Proctor • Preston Reed • Ed Gerhard • Martin Simpson • John Renbourn • Leo Kottke • Jacques Stotzem • Peppino D'Agostino • Jorma Kaukonen • Duck Baker

72 pp., $16.95
Item #21699222
ISBN 1-890490-13-X

RHYTHMS OF THE ROAD

Bruce Cockburn • Toshi Reagon • Don Ross • Norman Blake • Kelly Joe Phelps • Cheryl Wheeler • Peter Mulvey • Dave Alvin • Steve James • Doc Watson • Eddie Lang • Jesse Winchester • Jesse Cook • Eliades Ochoa (CD-only bonus track)

64 pp., $16.95
Item #21699229
ISBN 1-890490-17-2

WHAT GOES AROUND

Corey Harris • Mississippi John Hurt • Cats and Jammers • Bill Frisell • Muleskinner • Ricky Skaggs • Tom Russell • Edgar Meyer, Béla Fleck, and Mike Marshall • Dama • Patty Larkin • Paulo Bellinati • Janis Ian • Steve Tilston • D'Gary • Catie Curtis • Duncan Sheik

72 pp., $16.95
Item #21699180
ISBN 1-890490-121

HABITS OF THE HEART

Elliott Smith • Chris Whitley • David Grier • Guy Davis • Mike Dowling • Stephen Fearing • Laura Love • Josh White • Jerry Douglas • Merle Travis • Roy Rogers • Dan Bern • Kristin Hersh • Scott Tennant • Jim Croce

64 pp., $16.95
Item #21699182
ISBN 1-890490-164

ALTERNATE TUNINGS GUITAR COLLECTION

David Wilcox • David Crosby with CPR • Sonny Chillingworth • John Cephas and Phil Wiggins • Ani DiFranco • Alex de Grassi • Dougie MacLean • Ledward Kaapana • Trian • Peter Finger • Mary Chapin Carpenter • Paul Brady

64 pp., $16.95
Item #21699239
ISBN 1-890490-27-X

HIGH ON A MOUNTAIN

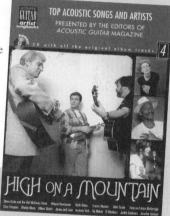

Steve Earle and the Del McCoury Band • Wayne Henderson • Beth Orton • Franco Morone • Nick Drake • Kate and Anna McGarrigle • Clive Gregson • Woody Mann • Gillian Welch • Jones and Leva • Andrew York • Taj Mahal • El McMeen • Judith Edelman • Jennifer Kimball

72 pp., $16.95
Item #21699195
ISBN 1-890490-09-1

ACOUSTIC GUITAR ARTIST SONGBOOK, VOL. 1

Sérgio Assad • Duck Baker • Doyle Dykes • Steve Earle* • Beppe Gambetta • Vince Gill • John Wesley Harding • Michael Hedges* • Philip Hii • Robyn Hitchcock • Jewel* • Pat Kirtley • Earl Klugh • Mike Marshall • Pat Metheny • Keb' Mo'* • Scott Nygaard • Pierce Pettis • Kelly Joe Phelps • Chris Proctor • Andrés Segovia • Martin Simpson • Tim Sparks • Jorge Strunz • Toru Takemitsu • Townes Van Zandt • Gillian Welch • Paul Yandell

100 pp., 2 CDs, $29.95
Item #21699216
ISBN 1-890490-03-2

* Not included on CD

At your music or book store, or order direct

Call   (800) 637-2852
Fax   (414) 774-3259
On-line **www.acousticguitar.com**

On every page of **_Acoustic Guitar_** Magazine, you'll recognize that same love and devotion you feel for your guitar.

Our goal is to share great guitar music with you, introduce you to the finest guitarists, songwriters, and luthiers of our time, and help you be a smarter owner and buyer of guitars and gear.

You'll also be getting the latest in gear news, artist interviews, practical player advice, songwriting tips, sheet music to play, music reviews, and more, every month.

Acoustic Guitar Magazine wants you to be happy. Let us show you how with THREE FREE issues. So subscribe now without any risk at the low introductory rate of $23.95 for 15 total issues, and enjoy three free issues compliments of _Acoustic Guitar_ Magazine. You have our unconditional guarantee: You must be completely satisfied, or your payment will be refunded in full.

Three Free Issues!
Subscribe today
(800) 827-6837
Or, place your order on our Web site!
www.acousticguitar.com

Refer to discount code AGBK00